PREACHING FROM
THE CATHEDRALS

MOWBRAY PREACHING SERIES

PREACHING FROM
THE CATHEDRALS

Edited by
HORACE DAMMERS

MOWBRAY

Mowbray
A Cassell imprint
Wellington House, 125 Strand, London WC2R 0BB
PO Box 605, Herndon, VA 20172

First published 1998

British Library Cataloguing-in-Publication Data
A catalogue record for this book is available from the British Library.

ISBN 0-264-67453-7

The quotations from W. H. Auden, 'For the Time Being' on p. 54 and Edwin Muir, 'The Transfiguration' on p. 80 are used by permission of Faber and Faber Ltd.

Typeset by Keystroke, Jacaranda Lodge
Printed and bound in Great Britain by Biddles Ltd, Guildford and King's Lynn

CONTENTS

*In affectionate and respectful remembrance of
six bishops in whose dioceses the editor has served:
Norman Sargant; A. G. Jebaraj;
Leslie Hunter; Cuthbert Bardsley;
Oliver Tomkins; John Tinsley*

FOREWORD

Cathedrals have been described as sermons in stone, expressions of the engagement between humanity and divinity. They assert, often in the centres of cities, the spiritual affirmations of men and women and the divine determination to nourish and renew self-giving love. Their architecture, art, music and the daily practice of prayer and devotion plead for attention even in the most secular surroundings and from the most hurried visitor. People find in cathedrals a space for mystery and thought, a sense of generosity and subtlety in life, with time to wonder. Here you can come in half-faith, searching for friendship, healing, wisdom and grace.

We can catch a vision of the Spirit of Christ in this great company of people in an ancient sermon. Preaching on Easter Day 1617, in Durham Cathedral, before the King, Bishop Lancelot Andrewes imagined all humanity embarked on a vast ship 'having their course through the main ocean of the world bound for the Port of Eternal Bliss. And in this great Carrick, among the sons of men, the Son of Man became also a passenger' (Lancelot Andrewes, *Sermons*, 1641 edition, p. 512).

Andrewes' vision of Christ present among all humankind should inform cathedral sermons, which may well address a wide spectrum of people. In parish sermons, the preacher knows personally the members of the congregation and is personally known by them. Their mutual pastoral care, in good situations, establishes credibility. These sermons are more broadly based, but I believe they are not short on humanity and relevance, nor lacking in concern with the deepest realms of the spirit. They depend upon the insight, honesty and learning of the preacher, and the willingness of the congregation to listen with sympathy and a critical intelligence.

This selection hints at the ecumenical mood of cathedrals as the century ends. Though most of the preachers are members of the Church of England, our colleagues include members of the Church of Scotland, the Methodist Church, the Roman Catholic Church and an American Episcopalian. The fresh air now surrounding cathedral relationships was sensed by the Taizé Community visiting London with 25,000 young people in 1987. They linked the worship and preaching in Westminster Abbey, Westminster Cathedral, the Methodist Central Hall and St Paul's Cathedral, so that a truly joint act of worship was shared. Ten years later, day-to-day relationships throughout the country continue to improve.

It is unfortunate that there are not yet any women deans in England, and I trust that this will be remedied before long. Certainly some of the sermons with most depth, clarity, humanity and humour are preached by women residentiary canons and other women preachers.

A clearer view of what makes a good sermon is outlined by Dean Tom Baker, who has given many years of his life to training clergy. Sermons, he suggests, should be

warmly human in manner and approach. The preacher should not allow the sermon to become just one more part of an excessively Biblical service. He or she should avoid the hieratic tones of the Liturgy itself and be sparing in Biblical allusions and begin where people are . . . not concerned with the niceties of ritual and ceremonial, but with the plight of the homeless, the underprivileged, the oppressed and the starving . . . [and with] the current crisis of faith and understanding.
(See James Butterworth (ed.), *The Reality of God*, 1988)

Writing this Foreword on the 25th anniversary of Bloody Sunday, one realizes how much churches in the United Kingdom, and especially perhaps the established Church of England, ought to be concerned with the tragedies and joys of our national history. And victimized minorities have been remembered: at Durham, famously, the miners and their communities; at Manchester, sufferers from our immigration laws; at Norwich, the homeless; in London, the victims of apartheid; in Southwark, the gay community. Cathedrals are also great centres for celebration – Canterbury celebrating the ministries of women, St Albans and other cathedrals honouring the work of their craftsmen and women. A full list would be enormous.

We have inherited a tradition of preaching which is profound and personal. John Donne's words are quoted wherever English is spoken and still make a moral demand which our politics hesitate to address. 'No man is an Island, entire of itself . . . any man's death diminishes me, because I am involved in Mankind; And therefore never send to know for whom the bell tolls; It tolls for thee.' The words of Cranmer, Shakespeare and the Caroline preachers and poets inspired T. S. Eliot, whose sermon in *Murder in the Cathedral* rings true in our age of many martyrs. It is significant that three of the most compelling English priests have been preachers who have drawn on our literary heritage – Harry Williams, Alan Ecclestone and Eric James. (For this literary tradition, see A. Ecclestone, *Gather the Fragments*, ed. Jim Cotter, Cairns Press, 1993.)

With such an inheritance it is not surprising that cathedral sermons are sometimes accused of *folie de grandeur*. The architecture of Chartres, Notre Dame and Durham, the music, the bells, the windows, the sense of continuity and space may lure congregations and preachers into unreality. They become over-conscious of 'excellence' and 'standards' and erect turnstiles in their hearts and minds as well as at their doors. These exclude the poor, the shy, the hesitant and those who are wracked with uncertainty over faith. Thank God today for the ministries of reconciliation at the

Metropolitan and Anglican cathedrals in Liverpool, recorded here in the sermon on Derek Worlock. Understanding and knowledge, not crusades or confident dogmatism, should mark our relations with other people and other faiths, as John Drury suggests in respect of Prince Hassan's sermon at Christ Church.

In all cathedrals, dignity has its dangers. One American bishop, John Coburn of Massachusetts, feeling the *de haut en bas* status of the pulpit of St Paul's, high above the congregation, dispelled any misplaced reverence by declaring 'This feels as if I were preaching from Brooklyn Bridge'. And I was present and felt the amusement when a canon of Lincoln, much oppressed by the finances of that superlative minster, inverted the Cranmerian phrase and prayed to the God 'whose mercy it is always to have property'.

Lay people tend to regard sermons as an inevitable ingredient of worship, to be borne rather than savoured. As long ago as 1624 a country woman commented that 'When the sermon came it would be such a bibble-babble that I am weary to hear it, and sit in my seat and take a good nap' (see F. Fernández-Armesto and D. Wilson, *Reformation*, Transworld, 1996). The same feeling is expressed in the twentieth-century story, possibly apocryphal, of the happily married priest who discovered a secret drawer in his wife's desk, containing two eggs and £2,000 in cash. On enquiry, his wife replied 'Well, when we got married I resolved that whenever you preached a poor sermon I would put an egg in that drawer'. 'But why the £2,000?' 'Every time there were a dozen eggs, I sold them.'

But a sermon has still a real function in stimulating thought, reflection and devotion. Members of a congregation today expect the preacher to aid them in their life-long search for truth – truth about God, about the Church, about themselves. Such a sermon may illuminate the figure of Christ, or enable a better understanding of one's own inner depths. Peter Baelz, the author of two of these sermons, speaks of 'entering into a conversation [with the congregation] which will lead God knows where. And if he knows where, and our times are in his hand, then perhaps we may leave to him the outcome of this peculiar but far-reaching ministry'. (See *The Weight of Glory*, ed. D. W. Hardy and P. H. Sedgwick, 1991.)

It is noticeable that recent studies of cathedrals (e.g. *Norwich Cathedral 1096–1996*) and the exhibitions mounted at cathedrals tend to be limited to the fabric, music and liturgy, with little attention to the theology, philosophy and beliefs of the period surveyed. The words 'sermon' or 'preaching' may not even occur in the index. This collection of sermons tries to answer the important question 'What did they believe in the last decades of the century before the Millennium?'

Cathedral preachers at their best have proclaimed the essence of the gospel to all their fellow-passengers. They have not shirked the difficulties and scandals of the gospel, but sought to share them with hearers who are church-goers or not, half-believers and searchers, as well as those who feel at home within the tradition. Preachers must always risk ridicule with the sophisticated, but will return to confront their questions again and again.

The sermons in this volume, so various in occasion and content, all reflect the same conviction – that the Spirit would give everyone the gifts of the Spirit: love, joy, peace, patience, kindness, goodness, trustfulness, gentleness and self-control. Cathedrals are open to all, and in the years ahead the Word in worship will continue to explore the paths of providence for each of us and God's destiny for all humanity.

Alan Webster

INTRODUCTION

The Exhibition of Sculpture at Bristol Cathedral in October 1979, in support of Amnesty International, included works by such famous names as Elisabeth Frink and Barbara Hepworth. A distinctive feature, however, was a number of works by artists who themselves had been prisoners of conscience. One such South African opponent of apartheid told me how he had maintained his morale over two years of solitary confinement by making sculptures from part of his bread ration. Another, Naomi Blake, who had been in Auschwitz as a young Jewish girl, was walking with me down the nave when she said 'I love this place. I suppose it is because prayer has been offered here for a thousand years. I would like to give you a sculpture.'

Her sculpture of *The Refugee* was set up in the cathedral grounds and dedicated at a service to which, and to a reception afterwards, members of the local Orthodox synagogue were invited. Representing a mother and child, it inevitably reminds Christians of Mary and Jesus, those Jewish refugees in Egypt.

I tell this story to illustrate the silent ministry of the cathedral building itself, prompting acts of generosity and love; the role of the cathedral in inter-faith relationships; the cathedral as a modest patron of the arts; the cathedral in support of the oppressed, prisoners of conscience, refugees, the desperately poor. I believe that most cathedrals have many such tales to tell.

The aim which I proposed to the publishers for this book

was conveyed to the prospective contributors as follows:

1. To proclaim the word of God for the edification of the readers. This has to be the primary aim of any book of sermons.
2. To illustrate the positive contribution of cathedrals today to the wellbeing of both church and state. In a church which traditionally exalts the parish as the focus of ministry and mission this contribution is often overlooked. Cathedrals still suffer from a Trollopian stereotype, as coverage of the sorry Lincoln affair reveals.
3. As it is recognized that cathedrals set a standard of excellence in the musical component of liturgy, so we dare to hope that we can demonstrate a similar standard in the preaching component.
4. To assert the value of the sermon as a means of communicating the gospel. As an institution, the sermon has suffered a serious decline in esteem over the last decades.
5. To strike an ecumenical note, as we hope to include a contribution both from the Church of Scotland and from the Roman Catholic Church. (Subsequently, the invitation to contribute was extended to a Methodist and a Lutheran preacher.)
6. To set a precedent for other groups whose value may not have been fully recognized. For instance, we would like to propose a similar volume of sermons by women priests and ministers.

I am most grateful to all the contributors for their prompt and effective response to my request for sermons and, in particular, to Alan Webster for his foreword and his encouragement throughout. This enterprise has proved a very happy opportunity to renew old friendships and make one or two new ones. Some sent one sermon, some two, some three or four. I have had to reject some good ones as well as not even approach some excellent preachers. In the end, I decided not to accept more than two from any contributor.

Horace Dammers

1997

1. THE FUTURE OF CATHEDRALS

(A sermon preached in Winchester Cathedral on 20 June 1993, as part of the celebration of the 900th Anniversary, by The Very Revd Dr Edward H. Patey, Dean of Liverpool, 1964–82)

I am to speak about the future of cathedrals – not an easy task because the future is always uncertain.

I do not suppose that the boys of The Pilgrims' School who are here this morning are greatly interested in the future of any cathedral, not even Winchester. But suppose that one of them decided to come back here in 50 years' time to have a look at the old school, and were to come into the cathedral to have a walk round, and perhaps come to a Sunday morning service, would he find things here very much the same, or a bit different, or changed beyond recognition?

That question can be looked at in another way. Suppose that, by some strange happening, this cathedral were to disappear overnight, leaving no trace of it behind. What difference would it make? Certainly an architectural masterpiece would be lost. So would a much-valued tourist attraction that has brought fame and finance to your city. But would it *really* matter? Would it matter in terms of bringing the gospel of Jesus Christ to those who live here or visit here? Could not the other churches in the city and diocese continue the job quite adequately, even if the cathedral were no longer here?

And if the cathedral ceased to be here, would it be worth rebuilding, and for what purpose? How much of what goes on here would you want to recreate in a new building? How much of what goes on here would you thankfully be rid of?

I, with four other priests, had to face questions of that kind when, in 1958, the Bishop of Coventry invited the five of us to meet him beside the ruins of his old cathedral that had been destroyed by German bombs. Pointing to the walls of the new cathedral, which were then beginning to rise a few feet off the ground, he said to us 'I want you five to launch this new cathedral'. From the time of that meeting, it took nearly five years to complete the building. During those years, our whole perspective was to discover how to plan for the as-yet-uncompleted cathedral that, in time, would come into action.

We discovered that we had to meet head-on two dangers that I think all cathedral people have to face. The first was the danger of cutting loose from the great heritage from the past. The second was the danger of being imprisoned in the past, and so being paralysed by it.

As we think of the future of cathedrals, we have to ask what good things must be carried into the future, even if in the course of time they may take very different forms. And we have to ask what things must be discarded.

I begin with my belief that cathedrals must continue to be centres of excellence in an age when so much is shoddy and trivial and the slipshod and the second-rate are so easily tolerated – even in the Church of England. Cathedrals must continue to stand out as workshops of creativity where language is beautifully spoken, music composed and carefully prepared, liturgy sensibly ordered and, in the name of the Creator God, art and drama can find purposeful expression.

This means the continuation into the future of all that is best in the cathedral liturgical tradition. But here, at all costs, the antiquarian, the stuffy and pompous must be weeded out and ceremonial symbolism which is now meaningless discarded when it has obviously passed its sell-by date. Even now we need to find new ways of expressing our faith, in creed and worship, in ways appropriate to the thought forms and art forms of our own times. This must be a major task for cathedrals in the future.

Because a great church like this comes most alive when people in their search for truth, beauty and goodness are permitted to 'do their own thing' within its walls, poets, painters, actors, dancers, musicians, from all sections of the community and with many different kinds of faith (or none), must be able to find a welcome and encouragement to explore and pioneer alternative forms of expression and worship alongside the regular and more formal life of the cathedral's liturgy. Cathedrals of the future must be seen and used by all sorts of people, not as a closed shop but as an open house.

Next, cathedrals of the future must find ways of organizing their personnel in such a way that they give a clear example to our divided and pluralistic society of how a mixed body of Christians can work together in harmony in spite of all their differences of outlook and personality. Most deans (I guess the best ones!) are strongly individualistic. Their role requires them to lead a body of men (and I greatly hope, before long, women) who are appointed as residentiary canons on the strength of their proven ability as theologians, teachers, administrators and pastors. It is well known that not all deans and chapters in all cathedrals live in love and charity with one another in the close. A future task for cathedrals is to discover better ways of appointing dignitaries, revising statutes and deploying staff to achieve the most effective and creative teamwork in cathedral leadership. There is still much work to be done here.

The community aspect of cathedral life needs to be developed by including in its decision-making process more lay people in what is still largely a clerical monopoly, and more women in what continues to look like a masculine stronghold.

And I can see the time coming when cathedrals must begin to take much more seriously the ecumenical dimension, with clergy and laity from other Christian traditions taking an increasingly prominent role both in decision-making and in ministry, not 'by kind permission of the dean and chapter' but by right as fellow-workers in the church of Jesus Christ. In this way, the cathedral, as the great church of the area by virtue of its size and past history, can become the centre point of the whole Christian mission in its district with an ecumenical staff to do it.

Within this wider concept of mission, cathedrals in the future will have to take a fresh look at their traditional role as centres of teaching and learning. There are too many people today who long to become believing and committed Christians, but who are put off by much popular evangelism and shallow preaching, by what a Roman Catholic writer has described as 'the temptation to offer processed food, easy sentiments, slogans and jingles' – Mickey Mouse religion! If the churches in England are to survive into the next century, which is certain to bring with it huge new challenges in science, technology, economics, ecology and community development, and if they are to avoid becoming more and more irrelevant sects on the edge of the real life of the nation, there must be, among the laity a well as the clergy, a re-discovery of serious theological thought. Apart from a few universities, where can they expect to find this if not in cathedrals?

No less important, the cathedrals of the future must become places of prophecy. There is a general expectation that those who run cathedrals, and those who worship regularly in them, are people who are by nature conservative and prefer to 'play safe'. But cathedrals with their high profile in the public eye should be places where strong challenges to contemporary values are made plain – not only by word but also by practical political and social outreach. This is not always popular among cathedral friends and supporters, but risks have to be taken, criticism about 'mixing politics with religion' encountered and unpopularity accepted as the necessary sign that cathedral people are living in the real world, because they are taking seriously the prayer that the kingdom of God must come 'on earth'. Even in cathedrals, the word of God (as the New Testament reminds us) is 'sharper than a two-edged sword'.

For all these, and many other reasons, I believe that cathedrals have a great future before them. They may even look forward to a bigger role in the life of the church than they have played in the past. The boy from The Pilgrims' School who comes back here in 50 years' time may find the cathedral flourishing in a new way. He will certainly find it very different.

2. CELEBRATION AND THANKSGIVING

(A sermon preached at Chelmsford Cathedral on 15 October 1996, at a Farewell, by The Very Revd Dr John Moses, Provost of Chelmsford, 1982–96, and Dean of St Paul's, 1996–)

My dear friends, we are now God's children, but it is not yet clear what we shall become. But we know that when Christ appears we shall be like Him, because we shall see Him as He is.
1 JOHN 3.2

. . . it is not yet clear what we shall become . . .

Those who have been to Florence may well have seen in that remarkable city the four stone figures carved by Michelangelo for a papal tomb. As works of art, in one of Europe's great museums, they have one surprising characteristic. They are unfinished. They have shape and form. There is striving, energy, passion, pain. But they are not complete. It is as though the figures are still tearing themselves out of the rough stone. They contain the promise of what they might be, but they are still becoming.

Now, those who go back a long way and who have really good memories may possibly recall that those are exactly the words with which I began my sermon at my installation as Provost nearly fifteen years ago. I chose that text, I used that illustration, I began with those words, because the whole emphasis at that time was upon the development of the cathedral. There was a great sense that the cathedral was unfinished, not complete, still becoming. The reordering of the cathedral, which had still to be thought through and carried out, was to be the springboard for what it was hoped might be important steps forward in the life and work of this cathedral. No one knew at the time what it might mean in practice. It is, after all, only as people come together and engage with one another, as ideas are shared, as mistakes are made, as possibilities are explored, as opportunities are taken, that life moves forward.

We know that that is true for us as individuals. We know that that is true for the institutions, the communities, that we represent. And the sense that this is how life is, how life will always be – unfinished, not complete, still becoming – is something to be owned and embraced and endorsed. Because I speak from the standpoint of Christian faith, I have to say that this is how life is because this is how God wants it to be. If that is the case, then certain things follow that go somewhere near the heart of all that we mean by Christian faith and Christian discipleship.

First, let us look at ourselves. I am not the first to suggest that Michelangelo's stone figures represent a truth that is fundamental to our life as Christian people. We are unfinished. We are living, learning, questioning, growing. Stone figures bear the marks of the hammer and the chisel. We bear the marks of our own experience; and we are changed by it. We are not complete. We are still becoming. If we are still discovering what we have it in us to be and to become, we will take very seriously the whole of life's experience, including the questions that we cannot answer, the ambiguities and the contradictions with which we are confronted day by day. We will take them seriously and we will find a place for them within the framework of values and meaning within which we live.

The call is to enter into life: in practice, that means 'living unreservedly in life's duties, problems, successes and failures, experiences and perplexities'. And why? Because only then – and I quote – do 'we throw ourselves completely into the arms of God'. Life is a gift. It is not to be hoarded, protected. It is to be spent. The challenge is whether we have the courage – and, I want to add, the imagination – to enter into life with the mind and in the spirit of Jesus Christ.

Secondly, let us look at the institutions, the communities,

that we represent; and, of course, that must include the church. Every one of us who is here this evening is involved in one way or another in building community. There are so many things that we want for the institutions, the communities, that we represent and to which we belong. But institutions – like individuals – are required to listen, to engage, to be caught up in the conflicts that are unmistakably part of living in the world. We become – as individuals, as institutions, as communities – what we have it in us to be and to become only in so far as we engage passionately, critically, with the world in which we find ourselves.

It is as we engage with life that we engage with God. Attitudes of mind that are partisan, dogmatic, exclusive, sectarian are the kiss of death. And there is no institution – no community – for which this is more profoundly true than the church. Such attitudes are a denial of the Spirit of truth who leads us – if we follow – into an ever-greater understanding of the truth. It is after all in the world that we find God. It is in the centre of life that we find the meaning of faith. Members of the cathedral congregation have heard me say time and again that the most important thing this cathedral does is to stand in the middle of Chelmsford, with its doors wide open. But, of course, I mean not only its doors but also its mind, its heart, seeking to work with all who care about the meaning of living life together in community – the priorities, the values, the disciplines – without which we tear ourselves apart.

Every one of us is well aware of the culture of contempt that surrounds all institutions. We know that the church appears all too often to have lost its foothold in the affections of people. But the response is not to withdraw into the security of our little world. If we are to be what we dare to believe God wants His church to be, then we will live with risk: in short, we will try – courteously and joyfully – to engage with life with the mind and in the spirit of Jesus Christ.

And if I labour these things, I do so because there are pressures at work upon of us today which suggest that we must first protect and secure and defend. The pressure is to

8

sound confident, to look inwards, to discover our own strengths, our own resources. And there are certainly things here of which we must take account. But if we are seriously engaging with life, with the mind and in the spirit of Jesus Christ, then we will learn something of what it means to let go, to live with risk, quite literally, to give ourselves away. If the truth about Jesus is also the truth about God, then what is displayed in His birth and life and death and Resurrection is nothing less than the extravagance of grace, the fundamental principle of sacrifice. He is quite simply the God who hands Himself over to His creation, engaging with us quietly, patiently, but waiting upon our response.

> . . . it is not yet clear what we shall become. But we know that when Christ appears we shall be like Him . . .

Unfinished; not complete; still becoming. These words could still be used of this cathedral as they were first used fifteen years ago. They could be used of us – each one of us – at whatever stage we find ourselves upon life's journey. They could be used of the institutions, the communities, we represent, and most assuredly of the church. But then – let us admit – we are broken, incomplete, with our raw edges reaching – please God – always towards the heavens. It is my hope that a cathedral that dares to stand not merely with its doors but with its mind and heart wide open might be for all of us a symbol, a sign, of a way of living, a way of being, that is rooted in God who reveals in our Lord the fullness of His truth and grace.

3. A DEAN'S INSTALLATION

(A sermon preached in Durham Cathedral on 16 September 1989, at his Installation, by The Very Revd John Arnold, Dean of Rochester, 1978–89, Dean of Durham, 1989–)

A place for the spreading of nets . . .
EZEKIEL 47.10

Fishermen will stand beside the sea; . . . it will be a place for the spreading of nets; its fish will be of very many kinds, like the fish of the Great Sea.

The scene with which the Old Testament lesson begins is one which every cathedral chapter prays will never come to pass literally. Imagine coming through the cloisters for Holy Communion at half-past seven one morning and seeing water flowing out of the door on the south side, and then going round and seeing it pouring out on every side – quite apart from then wading through it till you have to swim. I could imagine the answer which my colleagues – old and new – would give to the simple question, 'Son of man, have you seen this?'

Like much of the Bible, this scene is not best taken literally, for it is a dream – the dream of an anguished prophet, sitting down beside the waters of Babylon and weeping when he remembers Zion, attempting through tears to sing one of the songs of Zion and to worship God in a strange land and without a temple. Amidst the misery and affluent corruption of Babylon, a militaristic and mercantile civilization whose gods are the stars of heaven and the idols of the market-place, he dreams of living water flowing from a restored temple, purifying and bringing life and sustenance, healing and refreshment to the surrounding countryside and the surrounding nations, cleansing the Mediterranean and the Red Sea and even that stinking cauldron that is rightly called the Dead Sea – dead because it only takes but does not give the waters of the river Jordan, unlike Galilee that is a live sea because it both takes and gives and is a channel as well as a recipient of living water.

This is a vision and an inspiration for us in a cathedral, which as Richard Hooker taught is for the children of the New Testament what the temple was for the children of the Old. This is the vision that underlies Newton's well-loved hymn: 'See, the streams of living waters, Springing from eternal love'. We will do well, in singing that hymn, to concentrate: on the purity of the water that flows from here; on the quality of our personal and corporate lives, seeking to conform them to Christ; on the preaching of the Word, drawing on the treasures of scripture, tradition and reason, which includes both scholarship and response to experience; on the sacraments; and on the beauty of worship, laying under tribute all the God-given arts, especially music. From time to time, we will have to discern the siren voice of the spirit of this present age and resist temptations to leave these things, to which we have been called, and go and do something more relevant or more marketable instead. Resist, not in an inward-looking or self-indulgent defensiveness but precisely in order to ensure that what is proclaimed here, implicitly as well as explicitly, is the Faith and not something else – faith in God and his love for mankind, faith in Christ crucified for that love and alive by its power, faith in the Holy Spirit who sheds God's love abroad. We preserve and sustain these things which we have received, not to keep them to ourselves till they evaporate like the Dead Sea, leaving only the stink of putrefaction behind, but to pass them on to others like the Sea of Galilee feeding Jordan, refreshed and cleansed, new every morning.

A cathedral is a place of mission, or it is nothing, for at the heart of the vision are fish and fishermen and the prophecy that 'it will be a place for the spreading of nets'. It has been the grasping of that point which has caused the great change in English cathedrals, including our own, in the last generation. Of particular significance for cathedrals is the injunction 'its fish will be of very many kinds, like the fish of the Great Sea'. We cannot let ourselves be confined to the village pond. We do better to take the Mediterranean, which was the largest sea known to Ezekiel, as our model. This is a recipe for a comprehensive church, comprehensive not just in the narrow field of churchmanship (though it is that), but much more importantly in the range of human personalities who are to be attracted and retained, and of whom the Northern saints in their manifold variety are such an inspiring example. Who could be more dissimilar in all but sanctity than Bede and Cuthbert, between whose tombs, like the twin poles of a turning world, we now live and move and have our being?

> Some there were like lamps of learning
> Shining in a faithless night,
> Some on fire with love, and burning
> With a flaming zeal for right,
> Some by simple goodness turning
> Souls from darkness unto light.

The emphasis throughout Ezekiel's vision on the purity of the water should not be taken as a licence for the kind of ecclesiastical puritanism which cuts out of the church whole sections of the community, and which cuts down the creativity and capacity for love and self-giving of those who remain. The problem with that kind of puritan view of the church is that it does not allow the tares to grow along with the wheat, it judges before the time and it puts in the sickle before the harvest. In a comprehensive church, such as a cathedral must be, there is of course plenty of room for puritans too, except where they would be in a position to exclude everyone else; and all of us may dedicate ourselves to the positive task of being channels for pure water, as St Paul wrote to the Philippians, 'by filling our thoughts with what is true, noble, just, pure, loveable and gracious, whatever is excellent and admirable' (Phil 4.8). Then there will be little room left for judging others, seeing motes and throwing stones.

For there is in Ezekiel's vision a strange and deliberate exception to the triumphant onrush of pure water from the temple. 'The swamps and marshes', he says, 'will not become fresh; they are to be left for salt' (Ezek 47.11). Without fresh water we die, but without salt our growth is stunted. There is a powerful word here both for the ecology and for the laws of ecclesiastical polity; and we should not be surprised, but rather give thanks to God who provides in strange ways for all good things, if the wider cathedral community contains its fair share of human swamps and marshes, so long as they are there as sources of salt – not sugar, but salt with its unique capacity for enhancing individual flavour. Salt is good, said Jesus, in a short parable which might serve as the motto of a dean and chapter – 'Have salt in yourselves *and* be at peace with one another' (Mark 9.50).

The rest of Ezekiel's vision you will know better in the form in which it is taken up, scarcely altered, in that marvellous depiction of the heavenly Jerusalem in the Revelation of John, at the very end of the Bible, with trees on either bank bearing a fresh crop every month 'because the water for them flows from the sanctuary'. Only at one point does John correct, or rather amplify, Ezekiel – again with a word for the Church of England in our day. The New Testament breaks out of the religious nationalism which was both the strength and the weakness of the Old by adding to the words 'their leaves will be for healing' the essential clause 'for the healing of the nations' (Rev 22.2). Cathedrals have a ministry which is international as well as national, diocesan and local. Permit me to resist the temptation, which is a strong one for me, to say more on this occasion about the international and ecumenical themes of peace, justice and the environment, which come into my mind whenever I cross Prebends Bridge and see 'in the midst a stream and trees on either bank'. Let me instead simply remind you that Ezekiel saw fishermen beside the sea.

So did Jesus. He saw Simon and Andrew his brother fulfilling the prophecy, for they were casting nets. But the story does not end there. Again, the New Testament fulfils the Old by amplifying it. A little further on was another pair of brothers, James and John, and they were mending nets. In the church, in a cathedral like this, as in the locality and the university – in Europe and in all the world – there is a variety of persons in a variety of relationships performing a variety of tasks, all of which are important. I cannot enumerate them now; but I can thank them, and I do with all my heart. In a place for the spreading of nets, some are casting and some are mending; all are useful. There is no cut and dried choice for us between mission and maintenance, which is a false contrast left over from the 1970s, just as the choice between the horizontal and the vertical was left over from the 1960s, and the choice between transcendent and immanent from the Middle Ages. It isn't either/or; it is both/and.

The word for mending, here, is a word which elsewhere is used for building up or perfecting the church. We need menders as well as catchers in our company, as Jesus needed them in his: evangelism must be followed by instruction; justification by sanctification; wear by repair and repair by wear. You do not mend nets if you do not intend to cast them.

We are not called to choose between the two pairs of brothers and their task – least of all to judge them. We can only give thanks for them, and note the one thing that, in all their diversity, they had in common. Whoever they were and whatever they were doing, they heard the call of Jesus and followed him.

> Jesus calls us! by thy mercies,
> Saviour, make us hear thy call,
> Give our hearts to thine obedience,
> Serve and love thee best of all.
>
> (Words by Mrs C. F. Alexander)

Amen.

14

4. THREE CHOIRS FESTIVAL

(A sermon preached in Worcester Cathedral on Sunday 25 August 1996 (the Sunday immediately following the Three Choirs Festival) by The Very Revd Dr Tom Baker, Dean of Worcester, 1975–86. The Festival, which lasted a full week, concluded on the previous Saturday evening, with a performance of Elgar's *The Dream of Gerontius*)

One of the great philosophers of our time, Bertrand Russell, once wrote a book called *Principia Mathematica*. He wrote it with a collaborator, his fellow-mathematician A. N. Whitehead. It was of enormous length, and so intricate and difficult that only six people are estimated to have read it, let alone understood it. Yet it remains a great classic of its time. Hold that thought in your mind for a moment, if you please, and now turn your eyes upwards to the vaulting of the roof. There, at the apex of the vaults, are some carvings, or bosses as they are called. There are larger and more elaborate ones under the tower and transepts. They are beautiful and intricate, and must have taken a long time to make; yet nobody can see them in any detail, and the craftsmen who carved them knew that nobody could see them. Holding these two thoughts in your mind, consider now the pianist who plays only for her own pleasure. She feels unhappy about playing when other people might be listening, or in public, because she lacks confidence and feels she is not up to it, yet she obtains great satisfaction in playing, even though she knows that nobody will hear what she plays.

Here then are some examples of things that exist for their own sakes and are valid in themselves, apart from considerations of usefulness or profit, and with little obvious benefit to others. These are the things that run counter to the climate of our time, counter to our enterprise culture with its enormous emphasis on results, on achievement, on competitiveness. No, I am not trying to voice an opinion on economics. For all I know the enterprise culture, competition, market research, league tables, performance-related pay, and all the paraphernalia of the free market are necessary for our prosperity. For all I know. But what I am sure of is that these things, if unrestrained, can easily swamp and obliterate concern for the things that matter most of all, the things that are valid in themselves, regardless of profit or reward, things like the book on mathematics that nobody reads, or the carving that nobody sees, or the piano piece that nobody hears. Without art, without music, without craftsmanship, without games and athletics, without fell-walking, and flower arranging, and stamp collecting, and train-spotting, life becomes diminished, trivialized and, in the end, brutalized. We need to cherish the things, the activities, the enterprises that are significant in themselves.

Now I have used the expression 'in themselves' several times. On reflection, that expression must imply some intrinsic characteristic that, in very various degrees, lifts them above themselves. It implies an aura, a mystery, an inner meaning, that may, in some circumstances, evoke wonder and awe. Whenever I am deeply moved by either poetry or drama or music, I know that I am living in some immense meaning surrounding me, something that points towards what is infinite, eternal and awe-inspiring.

In the language of faith, it speaks of the glory of God. That of course involves a leap, the leap of faith. There is no necessary or obvious connection between things valuable 'in themselves' and the being of God. But there are some things which serve as what an American sociologist has called 'signals of transcendence', and I suggest that some of the things valid 'in themselves' that I have been speaking of are among them. Johann Sebastian Bach wrote music prodigiously all his life. Of course he wrote it for profit, for money. It was his livelihood. No doubt he wrote it also to win fame and acclaim. Yet many of his scores carry the inscription 'To the glory of God'. Beyond all the more

16

self-regarding considerations, his music is written to the glory of God, and that is its ultimate and sufficient justification. And that is true of *all* our best endeavours. They may be undertaken for profit, or for praise. But it is the knowledge that *beyond* that they are done for the glory of God that brings the deepest satisfaction.

And it is this, I suggest, that makes *festivals* so vital to our social wellbeing – festivals like the splendid Three Choirs Festival that has just finished and in which some of us took part. Festivals of course are all the rage these days. Indeed, they are becoming two a penny and some are getting out of hand, it seems. That's a pity, because festivals which are well established, like the Three Choirs Festival, the oldest in Europe, or those which are serious in their intent (and serious is not the opposite of popular), fulfil a vital social function. They are able to lift us above the level of the humdrum and ordinary on which we live most of our lives, and on to the level of the sublime, the level of joy, the deeply serious or the gloriously comic. Still more to the point, they are able to turn our attention beyond a concern for gain or profit, and towards what we have been calling the things that matter in themselves, that are significant for their own sakes, that point towards the eternal, that are taken in hand to the glory of God. So we do right to be grateful to those who contributed to making last week's festival such an inspiration. We do right to hope that festivals of this kind flourish and abound. Of course there has to be no small measure of commercialism in all forms of festival in today's world. It is inevitable. Happily, in the Three Choirs Festival there is still a strong element of the voluntary, of the local and of community spirit. For if the spirit of commercialism prevails altogether, the festival loses its soul, and becomes a self-contradiction. It must also follow that when a festival, like the one that has just finished, has an overt religious origin and a partly religious content, its capacity to lift us above the level of personal advancement, and witness to the things that exist for the glory of God, is all the greater. We must continue to be grateful. Let Festival flourish.

There remains a word of warning. A concern for art, music and drama can be pursued to the detriment of moral sensitivity. In a word, it can make us sentimental or callous. It should not be forgotten that Adolf Hitler and his murderous gang were, many of them, devoted to music, and sat listening enraptured at the Berlin Opera House in the full knowledge that at that same moment dozens were being tortured to death in the cellars of Gestapo headquarters just around the corner and that thousands were perishing miserably in the concentration camps not much further away. Beauty is supreme, but so also are goodness and truth. Sometimes a gap can open up between beauty and goodness. Such gaps are dangerous, and we have to mind them. God's glory was incarnate, not in a concert hall but in a human being, not in the philosopher or artist but in the obscure prophet from Nazareth, and the defeated man on Calvary, who inspired his followers to bear one another's burdens and support the weak. I have spoken of great works of art, music and mathematics as awe-inspiring – and so they sometimes are – but so also are words and deeds of generosity, tenderness and love. The Mass in B minor is indeed awe-inspiring – but so too is that definitive and all-embracing act of sacrifice and self-giving that the Mass is concerned to represent.

Maybe then it is as well if, as I return from the opulence of the opera house or concert hall or cathedral, ravished by the music I have heard, I am bound to pass on my way home many signs of poverty and deprivation – youngsters sleeping rough on the streets, and the squalid tenement blocks of the inner city areas – and am made to reflect on the disembodied voice of the London Underground warning me to 'MIND THE GAP'. This is in no way to diminish or qualify the importance of Festival, or to inhibit my enjoyment of its enchantments. But it may, and should, make me want to see such things more widely shared – to the greater glory of God, Father, Son and Holy Spirit. Amen.

5. THE ABBEY'S MINISTRY

(A sermon preached at Westminster Abbey on 7 July 1996 by The Very Revd Michael Mayne, Dean of Westminster, 1986–96)

'I just want a normal life', sings Adelaide in the musical *Guys and Dolls*, 'with wallpaper and bookends.' Well, so do I. And a small patch of lawn and a dog. And what have I got? This amazing Abbey, and a house with the portraits of twenty-six stern-looking former Deans on the landing.

I am quoting in fact from a sermon I preached on 7 July 1986, for today is the exact tenth anniversary of my installation as Dean. Now I am not in the habit of raking up old sermons, but because I am retiring in a few months I thought I would take a raincheck on just one of the questions I then asked about the Abbey and its ministry. My justification for doing so? These words in today's Gospel: 'And Jesus said, "Come to me all who are weary and heavy-laden, and I will refresh you. Take my yoke upon you and learn from me, and you will find rest for your souls" ' (Matthew 11.28).

And the question is: What do we exist to offer the thousands who come daily into this abbey church, some as tourists, some as pilgrims, some to worship, some to stare, many of them weary and heavy-laden, and needing refreshment? Those, like us, who hunger to be loved and to love, to be known and understood, to be at peace within themselves. What kind of a God, what kind of a community, may be glimpsed through our liturgy, our preaching, our music, the way in which we welcome strangers into our midst? How do we convey to them something of the transcendent mystery without patronizing God or reducing and falsifying those central, awesome truths on which the Christian faith is based?

19

For among those who come are many who are seeking for a faith that is intellectually credible and emotionally satisfying, the searchers and the half-persuaded. 'I believe our task', I said here ten years ago,

> is to preach and practise a gospel which speaks clearly, and in terms people can understand, of the powerful mysteries of our faith: of the unique, irreplaceable nature of each one of us; of the fact that God is in love with us and of that love and forgiveness as it is disclosed in Jesus Christ; of how we may recognize the signs of the Kingdom of God; and of the new life in the Spirit that may be experienced by those whose lives are centred on the breaking and sharing of bread in the Eucharist.

'Speaking clearly . . . about the central mysteries of our faith' and, in particular, about that deepest of all insights into the true nature of God that we find in Jesus who is the Christ. 'No-one knows the Father but the Son', says Jesus in today's Gospel, 'and those to whom the Son chooses to reveal him' (Matthew 11.27). So what kind of God does he reveal? What comfort has he to offer? Well, he puts paid to some of the more extravagant ideas of the Old Testament writers to whom God seemed an angry, vengeful, even spiteful being, his wrath in constant tension with his mercy, though Jesus' words are often far from comfortable. He denounces some as deaf or blind or hypocritical; he threatens others with judgement and punishment; he calls his followers to renounce purely worldly standards and values and seek the values of the Kingdom. He talks about losing your life in order to find it. Yet side by side with words that can challenge or cut to the quick there is a breathtaking compassion and a giving of attention to whoever is in need.

But this or that saying or healing is not the point. The point is that everything he says and does is said and done within the context of God's affirming love. That is the utterly new and distinctive truth that the Christian faith proclaims: that the God revealed by Jesus is love and cannot be untrue to his nature. That if you ask the meaning of your life or the meaning of Jesus' life and death, the answer is the same. Love is its meaning. He came to teach us what it means to love and what it means to be loved.

Now you *can* run a church by playing on people's fears and fantasies and the threat of judgement, and many do so. You can try and frighten people into faith. But that is not the way of Christ. For undergirding all his words, running through the drama of his life and death like a persistent ground-bass is the unchanging theme of God's love. 'Christ's proper work', wrote Martin Luther, 'is to declare the grace of God, to console and to enliven.' So Jesus invites all who will open their hearts to him: 'Come to me all who are weary and heavy-laden, and I will refresh you. Take my yoke upon you and learn from me, and you will find rest for your souls.'

And then his words cease. The voice that challenged the spiritually blind and entranced the sinful is stilled. But the act of declaring the grace of God, the act of love, continues to the end, and it is heard in all its consoling power in the final word of forgiveness on the Cross. And the last, most costly and most enduring word of God is just that: one of loving forgiveness.

And that in the end is what we have to offer those who come here seeking the one who may still be for them 'the unknown God', or the misunderstood God, the false God of their own fantasy. We have to offer one whose power is to be seen not just in the unimaginable beauty of his creation, but in his ability to change human hearts by the outpouring of his love and the enduring power of his grace, which we then experience as our true homecoming. And each of us will only seriously begin our Christian journey, we shall only see the point of prayer or worship or meeting for the breaking of bread, when we understand that we are loved by God more than we can ever know, and desire in the very fount of our being to love him in return.

6. EXPLORATION INTO GOD AND OUR NEIGHBOUR

(A sermon preached by The Very Revd Horace Dammers, Dean of Bristol, 1973–87, at St Paul's Cathedral, Calcutta, on 13 March 1976, during the visit of members of Bristol Cathedral and Clifton (RC) Cathedral choirs. It was later adapted for use in the cathedrals of Melbourne, Newcastle (NSW) and Perth, Australia)

Behold, I have graven you on the palms of my hands.
ISAIAH 49.16

It is great to be back in India. My wife and I spent four happy years in your beloved country. Two of our four children were born in India, far away in the south in the Tamil country. Now, it is a great joy to be visiting quite a different part of India and to be bringing you greetings from Britain. In particular, I bring you brotherly and sisterly greetings from Bristol and Clifton Cathedrals, the one Church of England, the other Roman Catholic. To those I may reasonably add Coventry Cathedral for, like your own Canon Subir, I have been admitted as a Companion of the Community of the Cross of Nails. On behalf of these three cathedrals, I thank God on every remembrance of you all, for by your work for and, what is more important, with the hungry and the homeless you have been showing us all what a cathedral can be and do.

I have brought with me a picture to show you. I am not sure how many of you can see it and in any case I would like to leave it with you as a small souvenir of our visit. It is a photograph of the great sculptor Auguste Rodin's study of hands which he called *The Cathedral*. Rodin was neither a Christian believer nor a morally respectable man. Yet God was able to use his great talents to his glory, and Rodin's *Cathedral* has much to teach us. It depicts a woman's hand and a man's sensitively exploring each other and, at the same time, aspiring, exploring upwards. As the work is called *The Cathedral*, we may reasonably interpret this upward exploration as being towards God. 'Thou shalt love the Lord thy God . . . and thy neighbour as thyself.' To launch out upon the sea of love, to explore how best to love the Lord our God and our neighbour as ourselves, is the mission of the whole church of God, and of cathedrals in particular. Let us look together more closely at Rodin's study.

These two hands, one male, one female, are representative each of its own sex. They represent the complementary opposites within the human family within which we are all neighbours: male and female, young and old, rich and poor, black and brown and white and yellow, the urban and the rural, the conservative and the radical, the scholar and the man or woman of action, the powerful and the powerless. Our ministry of reconciliation is to enable these and other complementary opposites to be reconciled in Christ Jesus. Of course this does not mean, and I emphasize the point, that our role is always to be neutral. No, our role is to be exploring the tension, discerning within it God's offer of reconciliation, God's mercy and judgement, never supposing that such reconciliation, such mercy, such judgement can necessarily be achieved without conflict. As a colleague on the staff of Coventry Cathedral once put it to me, 'When you try to reconcile opposites, you usually get bashed by both sides'. I know what he meant.

Now Rodin's hands are not only representative hands; they are also the hands of individuals. As such, they are sensitively exploring each other. Our Lord Jesus Christ was an explorer in this sense. So should his servants be. As we read in the Fourth Gospel, 'He himself knew what was in man' (John 2.25) and drew it out of him or her too. Psychiatrists today have rediscovered this wonderful human quality and labelled it empathy. The Roman Catholic Dr Jack Dominian defines it as follows:

By sympathy we share each other's unpleasant experiences; through empathy we have the capacity to put ourselves, in technical language to project ourselves, into the inner world of another person, recognise their needs, yet remain separate and so available in a way that their need, their distress or their love does not overwhelm us.

This capacity to project ourselves into the inner world of another person, recognize their needs yet remain separate and so available is as important in Calcutta as it is in Coventry, in Bristol as it is in Bombay. Christ had it to the full. How beautifully he entered into the inner world of the woman who washed his feet with her tears, anointed them with precious ointment and wiped them with her hair. Consider the equally notorious woman at the well in Samaria. (I know from experience that Christians in this country know their Bibles.) 'Give me a drink', he said, and put himself in her debt, precisely what she required, she whom respectable people despised and condemned. Remember too how he invited himself to supper with the hated Zacchaeus. Jesus was not playing psychological games. He was hungry that evening, as he was thirsty at the well. And his lonely soul needed someone lovingly to anoint him for his burial.

Even so when you invited my friends in these two cathedral choirs to come and sing to you, you entered into their inner lives. By the power of the Holy Spirit they have the gift of song which they love to offer to God. They have here an opportunity also to witness to the basic unity of the Church which is both God's will and his gift. So we have come. Please God we also are entering into your inner life. You don't wish to be thought of, in the West or anywhere else, as that city with so many dreadful problems, for yours is a great city, one of the world's great cities where life is lived abundantly with much sorrow and much joy, much sinning and much loving worthy of the best which anyone can bring or give, and with so much to give them in return.

It is as the two hands in Rodin's sculpture explore each

24

other that they enter also into exploration into God. Here too our cathedrals, yours and ours, have a vocation and a role. One obvious aspect of our exploration into God is public worship, what we are doing here and now. There is a striking passage in the Rule of the Taizé Community, that Christian band of brothers who work and pray so effectively for the liberation of humankind. It reads:

> Let us be attentive to enter into the meaning of the liturgical action; let us seek to perceive under signs accessible to our fleshly being something of the invisible reality of the Kingdom. But let us also take care not to multiply these signs and keep them simple, in token of their evangelical worth.

I take it that this means that our cathedrals' public worship should be as richly and deeply symbolic as possible, yet simple and straightforward enough to attract and hold those who are strangers to our Christian traditions and culture. And that's a big enough job in itself.

Then, secondly, our exploration upwards into God has to be by way of theology. I believe that a cathedral should be a centre of exploration of the application of theology to the great human issues of the day – poverty, population, profligacy and pollution – and also to the more local issues of the diocese in which it stands, for example local government, employment and unemployment, education, health and housing. About such matters I have nothing to teach you and much that I hope to learn, even in so short a visit.

Exploration into God; empathy with your neighbour, far and near; reconciliation between complementary opposites. Who is sufficient for these things? At this point, I turn away from Rodin's image of sculpted hands to another such image, set out in my text from the book of the prophet Isaiah. God is speaking to his people: 'Behold, I have graven you on the palms of my hands.' God stands, as it were, with his hands outstretched towards us in loving greeting, like the father in Jesus' parable welcoming home his prodigal son. But even more wonderful than that, he holds us indelibly and forever within the embrace of his love. Look, he has engraved your name, and yours, and yours, and yours, on the palms of his hands. In that faith we dare, in the words of William Carey of Serampore, to expect great things from him, attempt great things for him.

Now finally, my dear friends, for us Christians this wonderful image of engraved hands means more, far more, than either Rodin could grasp or Isaiah imagine. When the Christian philosopher Søren Kierkegaard was a child, his father once showed him a picture book of the world's great men and women. Pointing to the frontispiece depicting Jesus nailed to the cross, his father said to the little boy 'That is the best and kindest man who ever lived'. Snatching up a toy sword, the child, eyes blazing, replied 'When I grow up, I will kill the wicked men who put Him there'. 'But', commented the philosopher in telling the story, 'when I grew up I learned that I was one of them.' 'Behold I have graven you on the palms of my hands.' Yes, my friends, you and I are the wounds of Christ, gouged out by the bitter nails from his outstretched palms. It is at this very point when we recognize our hurt of him, our worldliness and lack of love, and offer ourselves to him in penitence and faith; it is at this very point that he transforms us into the visible marks and witnesses to the world of his undying love. Thanks be to God.

7. CIVIC MASS – PORTSMOUTH MILLENNIUM

(A sermon preached by The Right Revd Crispian Hollis, Roman Catholic Bishop of Portsmouth, at the Civic Mass at his cathedral on 4 February 1996. Bishop Hollis was the Administrator of Clifton Cathedral, 1981–87)

My dear Lord Mayor and Lady Mayoress, distinguished visitors and friends,

I have been long enough now in Portsmouth both to feel that I belong and also to take an active interest in the life and work of the city. I was particularly proud, therefore, to hear the initiative and energy of the city being praised to the heights by members of the Millennium Commission in London, when I had lunch with them the other day.

Your presentation has made a deep impression, and proof of that, if proof is needed, can be seen by the very substantial funding that is to be made available to the city to carry through its millennial projects.

In view of the fact that the whole celebration of the Millennium takes its origins from the birth of Christ – that birth that is the hinge of measured history and its turning-point – I make no apology for reminding our secular world that this is a time that Christians wish to share with all. In its origins, it is a Christian festival.

It will, inevitably, be a civic occasion of some consequence, but, at the same time, I hope it will be one when the city and the churches will be seen to be working closely together, so that it will be seen to have a very real spiritual dimension.

Coming, as we do, from a position that takes a particular view of the nature of human and civic society and the value and dignity of human beings, I believe that we, as your fellow-citizens, have much to contribute.

That being said, however, as churches, we will be preparing for the Millennium Jubilee alongside the city but with a somewhat different agenda.

This is a classic Biblical Jubilee, such as is described in the Book of Leviticus. The fiftieth year was always a very special time for social justice among the Jewish people, and it is from them that much of our own present-day thinking about the Millennium is going to come.

Some of the Levitical injunctions will make uncomfortable listening for civic authorities: for example, absolute honesty in all buying and selling, renewal in the understanding that God's laws are paramount, abolition of debt, abolition of slavery, generous sharing of resources – and the list goes on.

But, put in more modern terms, this means that the Jubilee is a time of reconciliation, a time of forgiveness, a time for sharing and a time for justice. Take on board all these things and we're faced with a massive programme of personal and spiritual renewal that I hope will be the agenda of the churches in the next four years.

The scriptures of this Mass today provide us with an agenda along these lines. Isaiah exhorts us to share our bread with the hungry and give shelter to the homeless poor, to do away with the clenched fist and the wicked word. Live like this, in the integrity of the children of God, and our light will rise in the darkness. We will become, in fact, light to the world and salt of the earth, and the nature – the basic nature – of light and salt is to be of service to the human family. That is our hope and ambition.

The question I want us to ask ourselves today is this: are these values, these aspirations, which can seem so exclusively spiritual and 'holy', completely incompatible with all that is being planned for our great civic celebrations in this city?

I suspect not, but I would urge you to give very serious consideration in your plans as to how we may better 'share our bread with the hungry and give shelter to the homeless poor'. I hope that you will set aside, in a named and publicized way, some significant sum of money in support of projects for the poor, the homeless and the unemployed. If you do this, I guarantee that you will receive great support and encouragement from all the churches. It will ensure that what we enjoy here in the city in 1999/2000 will not simply be a bonanza of fireworks and celebrations, but a real jubilee for the whole community – a jubilee in which the poor and the marginalized will be reorganized and helped, which will leave its mark on our city long after all the euphoria has slipped away.

'Heaven's light, our guide' is our motto – and it's not inappropriate to remind ourselves of that as the Gospel and the Prophet speak to us today of being light. 'Heaven's light' shows us the world as God sees it; it shows us our fellow-citizens as God loves them; it shows us the value and dignity of every human being, whatever the circumstances of their lives. 'Heaven's light' helps us see very clearly the presence of injustice, discrimination, inequality and greed in our society. 'Heaven's light' helps us to see the values which are rooted in jubilee and which need to be built into our celebrations of the Millennium – values like humility and repentance in the face of God's love for all people, compassion and love for the poorest and the voiceless, an urgent desire for reconciliation with enemies and the forgiveness of injuries and hurts, a thirst for justice and for a sharing of all the resources God has given us.

If we genuinely allow ourselves to be led by 'Heaven's light' not only will our celebrations of the Millennium be really memorable but also we will have become 'salt of the earth and light to the world', and everywhere God's name will be praised.

Am I being fanciful? Perhaps I am, but I think we are being offered a very special opportunity to do something extra-ordinary together, and we, as a community, want to be in the thick of that.

8. THE KIRKING OF THE CITY COUNCIL

(A sermon preached in St Giles' Cathedral, Edinburgh, by
The Very Revd Gilleasbuig Macmillan, Minister of St Giles'
(1973–) and Dean of the Thistle, at the annual Kirking of
the Council when the City Council attends worship)

The motto of the City of Edinburgh is 'Nisi Dominus
Frustra', abbreviated from the words of Psalm 127.1 –
'Except the Lord keep the city, the watchman waketh but in
vain'. Today, at the regular Kirking of the Council, the
question might properly concern us all: how far can we make
these words our own as citizens of the last decade of the
twentieth century? Are the words 'Nisi Dominus Frustra'
little more than relics of a vanished age of faith, reminders
of a simple confidence in a supernatural power that to our
culture is so alien as to be beyond the credence of reasonably
intelligent men and women?

One thing we should certainly not do is assume that our
predecessors – whether the person or persons who wrote the
psalm or the people of Edinburgh who chose the motto –
were naive or stupid. They knew that human effort was
required, and that God was not an alternative source of
power permitting men and women to switch off their mental
and physical engines, any more than Jesus was naive or stupid
when he said,

> Take no thought for your life, what ye shall eat, or what
> ye shall drink; nor yet for your body, what ye shall put on.
> Is not the life more than meat, and the body than raiment?
>
> Behold the fowls of the air; for they sow not, neither
> do they reap, nor gather into barns; yet your heavenly
> Father feedeth them. Are ye not much better than they?
>
> (Matthew 6.25–26)

The language is poetry and proverb. Of course sowing and reaping and watching the city are important. But much depends on the spirit in which these things are done, and the assumptions and perspective in which they are done.

If, then, human effort and divine keeping are to be held together, what does that combination mean for us today? What does it mean to be watchful for our cities and towns and villages? What are the threatening enemies against whom we must stand guard, like sentinels upon the ramparts of a fortified mediaeval castle? Let me suggest to you three themes which may go some way towards expressing both our need for watchfulness and our rediscovery of the element of the divine in human affairs, if we are to understand the motto of our city in living, contemporary terms – 'Except the Lord keep the city, the watchman waketh but in vain'.

The first theme is freedom and security, which of course go together. What are the dangers confronting civilized living today? Violent crime, emptiness of spirit, hunger, disease, fear, unemployment, rootless loneliness, hopelessness and other more or less overlapping interchangeable words? We want children to be free, and for that they need security – of course including the security of safe streets and parks, but also the security of a deep interior sense of belonging and significance. And we will not even begin to understand, far less solve, the urgent problems of crime and danger if we fail to grasp two things about us all: that we are communal as well as individual creatures, and that we are irrational as well as rational. Our personalities flow from past to present, from individual to individual, from judgement to fashion; and there exists within us all that element of the angelic and demonic which can express itself in the uncontrollably hellish side of our behaviour and no less in the gorgeously magnificent, generous, inspired deeds and words and thoughts. So long as people persist in the pretence that citizens are free-thinking, rational creatures there is little chance of the solving of social ills in this or any town.

I suggest to you that the more we open our minds and imaginations to the awareness of the messy mixture of

31

rational and irrational within us, and the extent to which we are both individuals and expressions of our inheritance and our environment, the more likely it is that we will be aware of the continuing stream of goodness that our ancestors called the providence of God.

There is a freedom of the spirit that cherishes the passing things of life without regarding them as absolutely necessary, and that freedom that cannot let us be enslaved to people or custom or things is the free dependence on God that is so like the liberty of a happy child in a secure home. To be watchful against the things that threaten that freedom and that security is a vocation to which we might all regard it a privilege to be called.

The second theme in relation to the wakefulness of the watchman and the keeping of the Lord concerns our attitude to the flow of time, from the past through the present to the future. Is there anything more important in a community than the upbringing and education of children? Yet wide as that is, it is only part of what should be for all of us a lifelong transmission of the culture of our predecessors through our experiment and development to those who will come after us. That culture involves skill and knowledge, and is both local and universal. One interdependent world requires security of home and a sense of pride in the wisdom, art, achievement and humanity of all races and all places. And it requires that same free dependence that becomes less trapped by the past the more it knows about it, more open to the influence of the new and the distant the more it loves its own little patch.

When they spoke in Old Testament times of the God of Abraham, Isaac and Jacob, I am sure they were doing far more than mentioning the happy succession of the knowledge of God through the generations. They were testifying to the sense that it was through their sense of the continuing, successive generations that their knowledge of God came (at least as an important element in their grasping of that knowledge).

To be watchful against the many factors that try to make us behave as people of a day, that diminish our sense of rich inheritance as citizens of the world with all its cultures, is not only a vocation to which we are privileged to be called but also a step in the direction of what our ancestors described as the living, moving, shepherding Lord God Almighty.

The third theme in thinking of our watchfulness and the Lord's keeping is what I call today Signs and Style. What we call The Arts is one aspect of a universal human characteristic, whereby people express their vision, hope and fear, their values and beliefs, in signs and ceremonies, in wordless music and carving and dance and gesture, uniting Grand Opera, a simple handshake, a crucifix, a kiss. Our western developed world runs the risk of developing some aspects of our humanity to the dereliction and demise of other aspects. The way we do things can be as important as what we do. The grace of God is not unrelated to graciousness and gracefulness, not unrelated to grace before meals or the grace of a cat walking along a stone wall.

To be watchful against the tendencies which despise and discourage that wide practice of sign and style in art and religion and simple gesture is a vocation to which it is a privilege to be called, and a step towards the rediscovery of authentic awareness of the Holy and Divine Spirit.

Today is Ascension Sunday, which, whatever else it means, affirms that the character and experience of Jesus are not left or locked in first-century Palestine, but are everywhere relevant and present. If you want to consider what things are worth seeking, promoting, defending, consider this list of attributes, and ask which of them best describe Christ the Lord: free, frightened, neighbourly, isolated, greedy, generous, establishment, radical, conformist, non-conformist, warm, cold, forgiving, judgemental, poetic, prosaic, dangerous, safe, doctrinally precise, spiritually open-ended, mysterious, straightforward, christian, human, divine, narrow, loose, clear-cut, suggestive.

Watchmen who are never off duty preserve a dull town.

9. A FAMINE OF HEARING THE WORD OF THE LORD

(A sermon preached by The Revd Dr John Tudor in Central Hall, Westminster at 'The Harvest of the City of Westminster' with civic heads, parliamentary representatives and community organizations, together with the regular congregation, in attendance. Dr Tudor was Superintendent Minister of the Methodist Central Hall, Westminster 1981–95)

The Central Hall is decorated with magnificent displays depicting the life of the City in so many ways. How indebted we are to God for the bounty that is ours. The supermarket shelves are overflowing. We have a superabundance of clothing, food and water – there is no wonder we sing with great gusto, 'Come, ye thankful people, come, Raise the song of harvest home'!

But with little imagination – because we are used to seeing scenes on our TV screens – we contemplate with horror the countries stricken with famine. The failure of food and water supplies sees a gradual ebbing away of strength and the will to live. Death comes almost as a welcome guest.

Amos was a shepherd who would know only too well the terror and ravages of a famine. In his prophecy he envisages a worse famine – a famine of hearing the Word of the Lord.

> I will send a famine in the land. Not a famine of food and thirst for water, but a famine of hearing the Word of the Lord. Men will stagger from sea to sea, and wander from north to east searching for the Word of the Lord and they will not find it. (Amos 8.11)

Now we have witnessed victims of famine stumbling towards relief camps, on the march to find food. Staggering, weak, undernourished, vacant. 'Now', says Amos, 'the victims will not be hungry for food but for the Word of the Lord.'

It would seem that there is a direct parallel between then and now. The tragedy, as Amos saw it, was that he lived amongst a people where the Word of the Lord existed but they refused to hear it. They had access to some of the Psalms, to the great tradition of Moses and Elijah. Amos' contemporaries were busy with nationalism, with the pride of state at the expense of other nations. They were obsessed with materialism, building lovely summer houses with expensive ivory while poor folk were sold for a pair of shoes. Theirs was a failed religion with pomp, priests and ceremony, but with no effect on moral and spiritual obligations.

We can draw a direct parallel with our great generation and times. Nationalism has reared its ugly head in the horrendous civil strife in what was Yugoslavia. There is tension in several countries in Europe over imported labour and the loss of employment for the native population. Materialism has taken over the world, with reports from the money markets being of prime importance. The quality of life today is judged by what we own rather than by what we are. Failed religion is sadly all too prominent with the churches failing to spread the Gospel, and clutching at each latest gimmick. Godless-ness is rampant, with a growing disregard for human life and dignity and property – all around us are the signs of a degenerating society. Little wonder that our contemporary society is so restless, staggering from one crisis to another, going for the latest theory or fashion. There is indeed a famine of hearing the Word of the Lord – and yet never before in the story of Christianity has there been available such a selection of such understandable and readable translations of the scriptures.

So is the outlook so depressing? Is there any hope on our horizon? We are celebrating the Harvest of the City, and we have gathered to give thanks to God. Here in the City the produce of our labours is not that of the farmer but, because we are historically children of the soil, we can easily picture

Jesus in a cornfield. He had looked on humanity in its desperate need of hearing God's Word despite all the trappings of his nation's religious life. He also knew the risk the farmer took when he planted his seed. He knew of the risk of proclaiming the true Word of God. He looked at the ripening corn and said 'The harvest is plenteous but the labourers are few'. Then he issued an invitation to those about him to impress upon their generation the need to hear the Word of God. He calls for the same commitment today – words that our society needs to hear, such as righteousness, peace, justice, joy, hope, resurrection and new life.

We, therefore, need two things.

First, we need to be articulate. We need to be effective communicators of what we believe. We need to put into our words the essence of the gospel, based on our reading of scripture. This is God's world which he has created and for the wellbeing of which he has given us responsibility. To be his stewards, we need to know his Son Jesus Christ who has died upon a cross and has been raised from death to life by the power of God. Through Christ, we reject those things which destroy our humanity and dignity, and we seek to establish a kingdom of his righteousness and justice and mercy. The scriptures declare the doctrine of the Priesthood of all Believers, so that the responsibility of being articulate does not just rest on the ordained clergy! Indeed, one very distinguished doctor of medicine came to a knowledge of God's Word through daily conversation with his tea lady. 'A truly lucid lady', he told me.

Secondly, we need to have an attractive lifestyle so that people can see the obvious effects the Word of the Lord has had upon our lives. Especially have we been influenced by 'The Word that became flesh and dwelt among us and we beheld His glory full of grace and truth' (John 1.14). 'In him we live and move and have our being' (Acts 17.28).

In my travels in the USA, I have heard some remarkable stories from the pioneering days. One comes from the era of the Gold Rush. Two gold-diggers were returning to the city and were caught by a blizzard. They sought shelter in a log cabin where an old man lived. He fed them and they told him their story. He gave them a corner to sleep in and hung a sheet across to give some privacy to them and himself. The gold-diggers were worried in case during the night he should steal their gold. So they planned a watch, with one sleeping for two hours and then a changeover. Came the dawn and the one woke and was angry. 'Why didn't you wake me to guard the gold?' 'I have slept too', said his partner. 'When you had gone to sleep I looked round the sheet and saw the old man reading his Bible. I knew we were safe.'

The Harvest of the City – not just to commemorate our physical wellbeing but an occasion to remind ourselves of the spiritual harvest to which our Lord directs us.

10. THE SOUTHERN CATHEDRALS' FESTIVAL

(A sermon preached on 22 July 1988 by The Very Revd Hugh Dickinson, Dean of Salisbury, 1986–96, in Salisbury Cathedral, on the occasion of the Southern Cathedrals' Festival)

> *Mary stood weeping outside the tomb*
> JOHN 20.11

Crucifixion was never intended to be an easy way to die. For Roman colonial governors it provided a reasonably cheap and simple way of executing criminals with such prolonged agony that anyone else contemplating murder or treason would have the likely consequences brought home to them as vividly and traumatically as possible. After one slave rebellion, the Roman Army crucified 6,000 men, many of whom took over a week to die. It is difficult to gaze steadily at this grim reality, as it is at the Holocaust: indeed we are inclined to wonder about the psychopathology of sixteenth- and seventeenth-century portrayals of the Crucifixion of Jesus by the painters of Northern Europe, who seem to have been determined to rub our noses in the hideous details of the torture inflicted on Jesus. And you would not, I think, welcome a preacher who forced you to look with any steady gaze at all that blood and pain. At least not today; on Good Friday perhaps. But not in the middle of this great Eucharist that is at the heart of our Southern Cathedrals' Festival. You might think it discordant, inappropriate, insensitive to the nature of the occasion.

And yet at the centre of this Eucharist, as of every Eucharist, from the grandest papal Mass in St Peter's, Rome, to the house communion in the kitchen of a council house in

Luton, stands inescapable, urgent and crude the bloody Cross of Christ. Yes, the Resurrection and the Glory are here too, but, as St Paul says, 'Wherever you break this bread and drink this cup you do show forth Christ's death till he come' (1 Corinthians 11.26). It is the pain of Christ that gold chalice holds: there's the rub. Blood in a golden cup. You can't get much more dissonance than that. That contradiction is an image of the dilemma that faces not only us in the Eucharist at the centre of our Festival of Music but also the whole of our culture. How do we hold together all this glorious music and that sickening picture of Calvary? Two nights ago, I watched and listened as Kiri Te Kanawa sang a glorious Mozart aria in Covent Garden. Behind her as she sang was lowered a huge, white crucifix on a crimson curtain: no blood – just white plaster. Was I alone among all those rich and powerful people in wondering whether both the music and the Cross were cheapened? Alone in finding my heart contract? The plaster image will not serve, neither there nor here. How do we hold together on the one hand wonderful concerts, great operas with expensive tickets, Impressionist paintings which sell for millions of dollars, eighteenth-century palaces full of gilded furniture and Meissen shepherdesses, all that beauty, and on the other men, women and children dying of starvation in the Horn of Africa, the atrocities of the Pol Pot regime, the sexual abuse of children, the undertone of violence and racism among us, the fact there are hundreds of thousands of people in our own country for whom the price of one evening out in London is more than they hope to earn in a whole week? How do we hold all that together? The question is asked not with the intention of making us feel a bit of preprandial guilt, but because there is here a genuine ethical dilemma, a question to our spirits, that to evade courts a sickness of unresolved moral doubt in our souls.

This is not simply the dilemma that we *also* face of living with affluence in the midst of world poverty. There is little moral ambiguity in the relationship between Dives and Lazarus: to feast sumptuously every day while men and women are starving at your door is plainly wicked. No, this dilemma is more genuinely perplexing. For the visual arts give eyes to the human race to see the world in depth; without the artist we are blind. To look out through the eyes of Van Gogh is to see nature on fire with God. As William Blake puts it, he enables us:

To see a World in a Grain of Sand,
And a Heaven in a Wild Flower,
Hold Infinity in the palm of your hand
And Eternity in an hour.

Music is the primal language of the human spirit. Beside it words, even the words of the poet, are narrow, stumbling steps to lift the spirit towards the realm of the transcendent. For that, the soul needs wings, and only silence has stronger wings than music.

But what does the music say? I am reminded of a story told, I think, of the great dancer Pavlova. On one rare occasion she danced a long extempore dance that moved those who watched her to tears. When she finished, a gushing admirer hurried up to her to congratulate her fulsomely. 'That was wonderful, wonderful', he exclaimed, 'but do tell me, what did it mean?' 'You silly little man, would I have bothered to dance it if I could have told you?' But still I want to ask the question. People sometimes say to me that they have no need to come to church to worship God. They can do that just as well under the blue sky and in the woods. But when I ask them 'Does the God you worship out in the fields have wounds in his hands?' they do not know what to say. That God out there is an ambiguous God. Does the God of whom our music speaks have wounds in his hands? We should remember that one of the commandants of the concentration camp at Buchenwald played Mozart every evening; and another used to pick out the string players from the Jewish intake for the gas chambers because he liked to have a string quartet to play Schubert for him. This tangled skein of sin and beauty has caught us all. For even as we sit and listen in this great cathedral, that is itself a kind of frozen music, out there the children of our human race are dying. Must we stop singing whenever a child dies, because Rachel is weeping? None of us would ever sing again. That is a way of letting the darkness put out the light. And must our songs then be only *Kindertotenlieder, Songs upon the Death of Children*? But for every child who dies two are born and we need songs to celebrate the birth of children. Yes, we need our *War Requiems*, music for *A Child of Our Time*; but the world is shot through with joy and glory, with tantalizing visions of beauty, with moments of heroic victory and sacrificial love, which we *must* celebrate if we are to be true to the rich diversity of our human experience. Celebration is part of the core curriculum of humanity.

And there, I think, is the nub of the matter. We must celebrate life, celebrate beauty, celebrate *The Planets*, celebrate the 'Four Seasons', celebrate the speckled 'Trout' in the mountain stream, sing some great *Song of the Earth*. But those great natural celebrations only find their true depth when they are heard against some deeper antiphonal *kyrie eleison*, the endless crying out of the children of our human-kind to God in rage and shame and grief: 'Have mercy, have mercy – Eloi Eloi Lama Sabacthani.' I think there is a danger of lovely words and lovely sounds becoming an opiate that numbs our painful sensibility to the agony of the world about us. Against that shocking picture of a Nazi commandant relaxing to Mozart after a day's work in the gas chambers, we must set another: a vignette of musicians, men and women in the death camps, who knew that they must die, sitting down to play the Beethoven quartets with all the artistry of which they were capable – as if to say 'Although we will fall into the darkness tomorrow, tonight we will make this affirmation of the light, this great YES to life and the human spirit and to God'. That music after the Holocaust can never sound quite the same. Holding together the beauty and the pain, the blood in the golden chalice, is the task of all great art and all great music and of this Eucharist. As Wilfred Brown once wrote:

It is my duty to stand in all weathers at the crossroads of human experience, assimilating all that I observe . . . so that my listeners may thrill to the articulation of something within themselves.

It is at the crossroads that the gibbet stands, and there Blake's wild flowers grow too. A singer open to that light and darkness will indeed touch the deepest chords in the human heart.

The music of a beautiful world; the music of a world in agony crying out in despair that great cry of dereliction. What then? Well, then a music that I believe only the profoundest religious visionary can hope to glimpse – the music of the End. Let me see if I can sketch in with these stumbling words the outline of that great final *Gloria*.

As we look about our world and its history, anyone of normal sensibility must feel that the sheer weight of horror, darkness and pain rules out for ever the possibility of the whole universe being ordered by divine love. The endless waste of young lives, the random brutality of nature, the concentrated cruelty of unavenged torture: there is surely no counterweight of our devising, not even the beauty of the world, which can be set in the scales of justice and of love to balance that hideous load. Unless. Unless the Cross and the unimaginable realm of the Resurrection that lies beyond the tomb are God's promise to our human race that in the end God has it in His power to make out of our human suffering a work of such glory and such joy that every man, woman and child who has ever lived can stand face to face with God and say to him from the bottom of their hearts 'Yes, Father, what we endured with all its horror was indeed worth it since it led to this!' My mind is too small to imagine what that great triumphant miracle of the divine love could be. But then I could never have imagined that God could make this miraculous planet on which we live out of the dead matter of a wandering star. All I know is that the God we worship cannot be God, who is the Father of Our Lord Jesus, unless he can work that final transforming miracle of love. No words, not even the Revelation of St John the Divine, can come anywhere near grasping that final glory. Perhaps the last movement of Bach's *Matthew Passion* looks into that eternity of peace and healing with clearer eyes than any other work. But even that amazing passage is no more than a whisper of the glory that will be.

Meanwhile, till he comes, we cry out our *kyries* in the faith that in our crying God's Son cries out and is answered; we sing our brief *glorias* in the faith that they will be taken up into the final triumph of the redeeming love of God; and so we hold together the pain and the beauty of the world. And with the blood in the cup we plead here the death and Resurrection of Jesus, claiming him as God's promise that in the end the darkness will not overcome the light. Despite the dark, we sing.

11. A CATHEDRAL FRIENDS' FESTIVAL

(A sermon preached at the Bristol Cathedral Friends'
Festival 1985 by Canon John Rogan, Provost of St Paul's
Cathedral, Dundee, 1978–83, Canon Residentiary of Bristol,
1983–93)

> *Do not trust in these deceptive words: 'This is the temple of the*
> *Lord, the temple of the Lord, the temple of the Lord.'*
> JEREMIAH 7.4

I was honoured to receive the invitation to preach at the
Festival of the Friends of Bristol Cathedral, partly because of
the affection in which I hold it and partly because a preacher
knows that here he stands in the midst of those to whom the
building is precious. The very stones of this Zion are dear to
us. Every year, people give of their time and of their money to
care for this temple. Whatever else a sermon should contain
on such an occasion, there should be a note of appreciation
for the endeavours of the Friends; and who better to sound it,
at such a time, than a member of the Chapter who is also the
Precentor.

But how have we come to such a commitment? Perhaps for
some there is some peculiarly intense event that has both
burned itself into our hearts and into the very walls of this
sacred house. The building is redolent of the freshest of
memories. With George Herbert, we say to ourselves that
here at least the memory stays fresh and green.

In addition, there may be the appeal of the composition of
the building itself. It is very fine: light, airy and spacious. The
proportions are good, and there is always something pleasant
on which to rest the eye and a sound to gratify the ear. It is
beautiful, and we respond to beauty.

For myself, there is the appeal of history, to know that so

much has gone on here for so long. Almost half the history of Christendom is enshrined in the fabric – and a good deal more in the artefacts that have survived, the harrowing of hell coffin lid in particular. I do think that there has been a Christian presence here since the twilight times of later Roman Britain.

And yet it is not always that sweep of the Christian tradition that impinges upon us. The Cathedral reveals its secret beauty in the Elder Lady Chapel, the Chapter House, and now, I venture to think, in the Sargant Chapel in the Undercroft – there, indeed, we are close to our tradition and to the great communion of saints. But these beauties must be sought out. It is the later nineteenth century that leaps out at us: the nave, the chancel screen and the reredos. The cathedral was singularly fortunate in its Victorian architect, whom we should always honour.

But whether the building had the most discriminating of friends is another matter. The Victorian era was in love with Gothic architecture. It was studied and classified: norms were established, to depart from which was architectural heresy. In short, the Victorians thought that they understood Gothic architecture better than those who invented it. Thus, good as is the chancel screen, the original builders never intended such a screen of that type. It was the Victorians who decided that the fifteenth-century people were in error; and they were right. The solid screen was removed and an open one placed in its stead. (But, with true sense of economy, the stones were used as wall fill for another part of the building!) While the abbey church was designed as a whole – a so-called hall church – for liturgical purposes, Gothic churches consisted of a church within a church. The choir was the church within. Since choir offices were the backbone of the worship, this was designed as a self-contained area. You can see the basic idea unimpaired in Westminster and Manchester. Bristol and Durham met the same fate and for the same reason: to open out the building for large popular services, in an era when people went to church in large numbers.

Again, mediaeval and Roman architecture used a good deal of colour: ornaments were painted and walls were colour-washed. We can see something of this in the Eastern Lady Chapel. But the nineteenth century thought this rather vulgar, and as a result we have the white and grey effect of the sanctuary. In common with a great many buildings, we have many fine statues, but it is hard to pick out detail because they lack the definition of colour. It may be that the twentieth century with all its great skills can find some way of completing what the nineteenth century began.

Our concern, however, is not merely with fabric but with people. The Friends reach out to those who seek the good of this place and who evince an interest in it. That means a continual attempt to recruit members; but it also means an attempt to relate to our visitors. Cathedrals are under constant pressure to respond to the tourist: indeed, there is general talk of a ministry to tourists. A certain reserve is needed at this point, lest we slip into a slick style in which we disguise the facts from ourselves, supposing it to be some form of ministry. Some parts of the Liaison Team Report of 1984 fed this illusion. There was talk of having a priest constantly present in the cathedral, fully kitted out in his cassock, so that people could not only be 'served', instantaneously, but have no difficulty in identifying the point of 'service'. Such expectations are unrealistic; and have never been met in any church of any denomination known to me.

Our visitors are the passing trade. They are like the sparrow in King Edwin's hall in Northumbria. It came into the hall from we know not where, rested a while, and then went out we know not whither. I watch the visitors while the Divine Office is being sung: they wander round and go their way. They gaze at the stone, the monuments and the ornaments, but the worship they leave on the other side. It is wrong to think that such people start to consider the faith on the basis of such openness. The starting point must be the ethos of the place. 'My house shall be a house of prayer for all people.' The concentration of a cathedral community upon the eternal verities, the direction of souls towards prayer and

46

contemplation and the serenity that comes from religious practice – these, I believe, are the things that might move people towards those things that belong to their peace in Christian discipleship. If we need discerning friends, we require spiritual companions.

Apart from the impact of the architecture, it is perhaps our music that might stir people to things divine, if they would attend to it.

We must admit that the ordinary English musical tradition does not relate easily to much that there is in the church repertoire. The ordinary visitor responds to the full harmonies and predictable melodies of the era of Sir Arthur Sullivan, rather than the polyphony of sixteenth-century Italy and seventeenth-century counterpoint. Palestrina and Purcell are composers for the Insiders. And yet, if people would give themselves time it could be accessible to them. Before most Evensongs we have a choir practice which is virtually a proto-Evensong. If the visitor listened to that, he or she would more readily enter into the worship which follows on so soon afterwards.

All these things we may regard as temples of the Lord. And yet I have chosen a text that speaks of them as deceptive words. Why is this? It is because the care of the fabric, the presentation of the music and the care of the people all depend on more than professional competence, in the pursuit of excellence. The mechanics are not enough. The letter killeth; the spirit giveth life.

We are deceived if we think that the topics I have mentioned are ends in themselves. They are not. They are means to an end: the great end of the service of God (whom we serve as a friend serves another). Everything depends upon the spirituality of the friends. Their commitment cannot rest in a commitment to stones and liturgy, but only in a commitment to Jesus as the Christ. That is the spring from which all else comes. It is a simple thing to say but without it nothing else is worth anything – however beautiful the building, warm the greeting and limpid the sound. As Paul said at Athens: 'The God who made the world and everything in it, being Lord of heaven and earth, does not live in shrines made by men, nor is he served by human hands, as though he needed anything' (Acts 17.24–25). Let us remember our place in the divine *schema*: a modest place it is, with the continual possibility of error and presumption. He has declared that he will act in righteousness through a man whom he has raised from the dead.

We are privileged to inherit the beauty of a building that has been sanctified by a continuous community down many centuries. The building is the shell for the devotion. As Solomon declared:

> Heaven and the highest heaven cannot contain thee; how much less this house . . . Yet have regard to the prayer of thy servant and to his supplication . . . And hearken to the supplication of thy people Israel when they pray towards this place; yea, hear thou from heaven, thy dwelling place, and when thou hearest forgive.
>
> (2 Chronicles 6.18–21)

That is our prayer for today – of high Festival – discharged with grateful heart and hands and voices. We pray for the peace of Jerusalem, glad when they said to us, let us go into the house of the Lord. And, today indeed, our feet are standing in his courts on this happy, joyful, festal day.

12. CHRISTIANS AND MUSLIMS

(A sermon preached on 11 June 1995 by The Very Revd Dr John Drury, Dean of Christ Church, 1991– , at Christ Church Cathedral, Oxford, on the Sunday after Prince Hassan of Jordan had preached there)

Last week, Prince Hassan spoke strongly and gracefully to us here in what he called 'this House of God'. His sermon began in the heart of Islam, as he invoked God the beneficent, the merciful, and ended in the heart of Christianity, with St John's great text 'God is love'.

As I listened, I recalled an incident from the time of the Crusades, those furious and terrible Christian onslaughts on Islam. An Arab writer paid a visit to a Christian church in Jerusalem. Puzzled by a statue there, he asked a Christian priest what it represented. The answer came pat: 'It is God in the arms of his Mother.' The Muslim was appalled, but too polite to protest. He went away reflecting to himself 'but God is greater than anything which the heathen say about him'. There is a good deal to ponder there.

First, there is utter contrast. Compared with last Sunday, a very polite demo apart, there was no meeting of hearts or minds, such as we enjoyed, in that mediaeval encounter. Nor is it hard to see why. The context was war and coercion – the things that Prince Hassan condemns and forswears, not only with his lips but also in his busy life. More than that, the invitation that we extended and he accepted was a positive turning of our backs on the sort of cold war between religions that some still favour. The positive peace of worship was our context: Muslims hearing our scripture and creeds, we attending to the beliefs of Islam, all meeting heart to heart – by giving each other the best attention – in worship in God's house. Context matters tremendously. Let us be thankful that we live in a local and global context that, for all the timidity and terror, at long last supports such an occasion sufficiently. And we can be thankful too that Christ Church has done its bit to confirm and develop that better context, assenting to the way of Christ who 'came and preached peace to you who were far off and peace to those who were near' (Ephesians 2.17). An institution like ours, so rich in Christian talent, is not meant to bury it or keep it in intensive care but adventure it in the world.

But back to the Muslim, the priest and the statue. The sad thing about that incident was that the context of force and fear in which they lived screened off from each of the participants the gifts of grace that the other had inherited with his religion. Probably they were both nice men, going about doing the good they could. Certainly each had in his mind the treasures of wisdom stored there by his religion.

The Muslim would have been possessed of the transcendent purity of the divine, beyond human words and concepts, such as we gathered from Prince Hassan. He had, too, that tradition of prophecy to which the prince bore witness – including Jewish and Christian prophecy, and all calling mankind to the way of justice and compassion. But the Christian could not realize this.

And the Christian priest had all that his statue of the Madonna and Child had given him, a sense of the humanity of God, the divine availability in terms of the most primal relationship of all our lives. It told of how we nourish and cherish another, of the joyous and trusting gaze that is the cement of society – at least of any society worth living for. So many prayers, full of need and love, had been evoked by that statue. And from it have flowed some of the most beautiful things we know in devotion, music and the peaceful arts. But the Muslim could not realize this.

So from that encounter before the statue, each went his way, shaking his head at the ignorance of the other – the heathen. The statue remained for a while, no doubt to be destroyed when Islam took over, yet another of beauty's losses to ideology. (At least nowadays it would have gone into the sale room or a museum.) And, as the Muslim knew, God remains for ever, over and above our ignorances and negligences, beneficent and merciful.

What, then, shall we say? We had better say something rather than let the precious opportunity, missed by those men because it was unavailable to them in their time, slip away untaken yet again. And it had better be said in the sight of God and, once again, in His house and ours.

Let me put it crudely enough to make a thoughtful Muslim or Christian wince: what do you think might be God's idea for all this? More crudely still: does God want one of our religions to triumph over its brothers and put them out of business? Would that be the thing to rejoice the Eternal's heart or vindicate the Eternal Wisdom?

Islam has already spoken. The Prince quoted the Quran: 'You have your religion, and I have mine.' 'Wherever God's caravans turn, shall be my religion and my faith.' And he was clear in his opposition to coercion, force, triumphalism and ignorance. 'Peace be upon you all.' It is not for me to embroider those clear words.

The Christian preacher now has his turn. A confession first. When Prince Hassan rehearsed Muslim belief that 'Muhammad is the seal of the tradition of prophecy, his message the fulfilment of all the previous revelations which go back to our forefather Abraham', I twitched slightly in my stall for, as a Christian, I could not agree. The difference between our religions is sharp and clear here. 'You have your religion and I have mine' – but this time with the temptation to say it a touch brusquely, not inquiringly or kindly. I steady myself by reflecting that Jews must feel much the same as I did then when we Christians blithely treat their religion as a superseded run-up to our own. And the Canaanite priests and people must have felt more than resentful when they were supplanted by Joshua's Jewish invasion of their ancestral homelands. Religious irritation and its reasons, among which colonization stands high, are worth knowing about. But it is not something to cultivate.

So, instead, let us address the question. In religion, in the

51

sight of God's justice and mercy and in His house, what is
superseded and what is ultimate? Christian theological
answer: human hostility is superseded, divine love is ultimate. To put it another way, superseding itself is superseded
if it has anything in common with that chilling utterance
of Nikita Khrushchev, 'We will bury you'. (They didn't, of
course, and now a task of the hour is to help the people
in the ruins of the former Soviet empire lead a decent,
basic human life.) But human supersession is always prey to
the destructions of the victory-seeking devil. Superseding is
God's alone. Our second lesson made this abundantly
clear: 'God has made him both Lord and Christ, this Jesus
whom you crucified' (Acts 2.36). It is never our business
in the first instance, never something for us to go for straight
out. Understanding and communion heart to heart is our
primary business. The supersession of ignorance and fear
will follow from it as day from night, and not the instant
application of main force and violence. We are here to make
the best of one another, and only so become wiser and less
frightened, only so supersede the dangers of darkness. It is
for one religion to understand and love its neighbour, secure
in knowing that to do so will refresh and clarify its sense of
its own value, dispel its fear and ignorance of itself. It is the
same amongst nations and between the groups within them.

There are, then, two kinds of superseding.

The first is part of the process of salvation and enlight-
enment. It can be experienced in a good conversation,
tutorial or committee meeting, as well as in religion. Here,
the participants seek together, helping and correcting one
another, what is true, just and humane. There is no talking
for victory, rather a common and candid participation in
seeking the good, in seeking the wholeness of the kingdom
of God, not our own partial power and glory. The supersession of cruelty and ignorance follows from it with the
modesty of patience and the easiness of grace – for this
supersession is a gift which comes from the goodness that
we seek, and seeking find – a supersession not grabbed
but given.

The second is part of the process of victory and revenge, devastation and damnation. Here, the participants are each out to win. Ignorance and fear are positive advantages to it, stiffening the sinews of hostility by means of a diabolical caricature of the opponent and the certainty that he will overcome you if you don't overcome him first. It follows from this that any triumph is radically insecure and temporary, for it is not based on the common and transcendent good but on tribal and base advantage. Necessity and force come hard and short – but the memories of the defeated are long. The conquerors know this and fear it: theirs is a supersession grabbed, but never granted.

In the end, we come back to what practically everybody knows. There is God, who is the ultimate. There is the human race, that is not. And the nearest we get to the ultimate is when a human being puts herself or himself at the disposal of God's beneficence, truth and compassion in service, not in self-aggrandizement. That is what all the statues, prophecies, doctrines, holy books and holy paraphernalia are in aid of. When it happens, anyone not totally blinded by prejudice can see it. So our Gospels tell us on every page. Beauty and charity are there among us to guide and heal. There is Christ with, as the Quran says, his 'guidance and light'. We are not entitled to congratulate ourselves on having that guidance and light unless we take it and walk in it, not to pride ourselves on having Christ unless we obey him, not to claim God as our Father unless we live with other people as our brothers and sisters, because his will is our peace and our neighbours' – indivisibly. And if we realize that and do it we soon find that we have a long way to go as well as enough bread to sustain us on the roads 'wherever God's caravans turn'.

Our own poet, W. H. Auden, wrote some lines on the Gospel text which says that Christ is the Way and the Truth. It is a text which comes readily to those who objected to what happened last week, because they understand it exhaustively and exclusively. Auden refreshes it by understanding it as a door, not a road-block, an invitation to explore, not to let fear stop the search for truth, and to find a common home in the city of God. Here is what he wrote:

He is the Way.
Follow Him through the Land of Unlikeness;
You will see rare beasts, and have unique adventures.

He is the Truth.
Seek Him in the Kingdom of Anxiety;
You will come to a great city that has expected your return
    for years.

13. CONVOCATION SERMON

(A sermon preached in the Church of St Margaret, Westminster, by The Very Revd Tom Baker at the Eucharist. It was attended by the full Synod of the Church of England, the Archbishop of Canterbury being the celebrant. The service was also attended by the Lord Chancellor and the Speaker of the House of Commons. The occasion was the seventh centenary of the Convocation of Canterbury)

> *Wisdom builds the house*
> *good judgement makes it secure*
> PROVERBS 24.3

The seventh centenary of this Convocation may be a suitable time to reflect a little on the Church of England today, and especially to ask if it has some distinctive 'gift of the Spirit' to offer, both to its own members and to the whole Church of God. Well, we could bring out of store many of the old treasures of which it has been proud, but some of these are looking a little tarnished now.

Yet there is one characteristic – dare we say, charisma? – that is still on offer and has not lost all its sparkle. 1 speak of the appeal to reason, alongside scripture and tradition, as a real source of authority. I speak of the conviction that, while reason does not create faith, yet faith must at all points be undergirded by reason. This general approach certainly had its antecedents before the Reformation, for example in the writings of Aquinas and of Erasmus. But it is in classical Anglicanism, and especially in the work of Richard Hooker, that it finds particularly clear expression. For Hooker, and those who follow his way, the light that illumines our path comes from many sources, not from one alone. The Word of God, he says, is indeed a two-edged sword – but put into the hands of reasonable men. He writes:

There is in the world no kind of knowledge, whereby any part of Truth is seen, but we justly account it precious – yea, that Principal Truth, in comparison wherewith all other knowledge is vile, may receive from it some kind of light.

This is the light of reason that, indeed, does not create faith but must at all points undergird it.

Now reason, rightly understood, is something far more than cold logic. Nor is it a sterile intellectualism. Certainly it possesses a rigour, an integrity, even an austerity proper to itself. But it also includes such things as intuition, insight, imagination, pastoral sensitivity and aesthetic awareness. It embraces also that elusive practical quality we call sweet reasonableness or commonsense. It is a faculty that has some affinities with that divine Wisdom of which we heard tell in this morning's Old Testament reading. I repeat, understood in this way, reason does not create faith, but must at all points undergird it.

The church needs the gift of reason as never before. We think of the pressing ethical issues of our time, on which neither scripture nor tradition can offer direct guidance. The question of nuclear armaments, that we are soon to debate, is a singularly poignant example. We think of the urgent task of speaking effectively of God and the things of God in a secularized society where the accustomed words and images have lost their resonance, even amongst some of us who use them still. Here, too, neither scripture nor tradition will carry us all the way, because it is precisely the words and images contained in them which are in question. We think of those sinister forces of deliberate unreason that have been present in the church ever since St Paul carried on that exasperated correspondence with his unruly flock at Corinth, and that seem to be gathering strength today. We detect in some places a tacit or explicit irrationalism, an unwillingness to expose particular convictions to the light of argument and an arrogant dismissal of theologians that itself betrays a contempt for truth.

It seems likely that the Church of England, through its Doctrine Commission, may attempt to formulate again its own positive teaching, in contemporary terms and contemporary style. Such an undertaking will be daunting and hazardous. But if it were to be successful, the result just might be a thing rare and precious, characterized by a steady appeal to reason, imbued with that mingling of conviction and tolerance, that love of freedom, that reticence and courtesy that is a trade mark, not only of the Church of England but also of the English people at their best.

The Church of England, like the English people, needs to discover a new and distinctive role, lest demoralization deepens. In the eyes of many, it must look rather like an elderly lady, all frills and flounces, set in her ways, stiff in the joints, not getting around very much, spending most of her time isolated and alone in her elegantly furnished drawing room. But not all old ladies are like that. Some are sprightly, shrewd, well travelled, adventurous in their thinking and with a lot to offer. What I am suggesting is that the Church of England does bring along with its history something precious to offer, a special gift of the Spirit, that comes from God. And it is something we do not value enough, and may even be in danger of losing. It consists in a quiet determination always to appeal to reason, alongside scripture and tradition, and a controlled passion for truth. It is not confined to any one party, and it is all the more potent for being much of the time taken for granted. Such a charisma is not showy, nor very glamorous. It lacks the attraction of the deep spirituality of western Catholicism, the sense of mystery found in Eastern Orthodox worship, the rigorous scholarship and clear definition of classical Protestantism, the warmth of fellowship found in the black churches, the ebullient enthusiasm of the Pentecostals and the political commitment of the Liberation movements. Let us frankly admit that, in the hierarchy of the gifts of the Spirit, it may not rank very high but, in a world poised on the brink of madness, it can come in handy all the same. And it is something we have to offer.

It may be encouraging to recall that in the religion of Israel the figure of Wisdom has humble origins in a down-to-earth, prudential ethic not unlike what we call sweet reasonableness. Yet it was this same figure of Wisdom that was at last exalted to become among the most elevated of all the Christological titles, being expressly identified with Christ himself, the Wisdom of God and the Power of God – to whom, in the unity of the Father and the Holy Spirit, be ascribed all praise and adoration, now and for ever. Amen.

14. THE FESTIVAL OF THE SONS OF
THE CLERGY

(A sermon preached at St Paul's Cathedral on 14 May 1996 by The Very Revd Michael Mayne, Dean of Westminster, 1986–96, on the occasion of the 342nd Festival of the Sons of the Clergy)

The first time I stood in this immodest pulpit – immodest, that is to say, by Abbey standards – was to preach at the installation of Eric Evans as Dean. Eight years later, almost to the day, I can't resist expressing our corporate sadness at the coming enforced retirement of this good and courageous man who has won the affection of so many.

The second time I stood here was to preach to the serried ranks of the United Livery Companies, many in their robes of office, and I thought 'Why me?' And I came up with no very convincing answer.

Now I face the members of this distinguished corporation and their guests and supporters. Part of your aim is to help widows of Anglican clergy and their dependent children, and this time I know the answer to 'why me?' for I am one. And I hope you will understand and bear with me if I take what my heart tells me is a unique opportunity to tell you a little of my story in unusually personal terms, for it is not irrelevant to why you are here too. And when I have done so, I hope you will know why, for me, today is rather more than just another preaching engagement in my second favourite church in London.

I am an only child, and my father was a priest, the rector of a small, idyllic country parish in Northamptonshire. He was older than my mother, whom he had married when he moved to his parish in 1928, and in the following year I was born.

59

I still have the old photograph albums, and all my earliest memories are of that delectable time: me in my pram, in the huge rectory garden; me taking my first halting steps clutching a stuffed rabbit; me on my first tricycle circum-navigating the rosebeds. My mother appears in scores of them, my father perhaps half a dozen times. And then, after a brief four years, the photographs come to an end for, on a Saturday afternoon in May, my father wrote a note to my mother, who was out, climbed the tower of his church beside the rectory, removed the boarding from the belfry and threw himself down. The gardener found him, but he died almost instantaneously.

My mother was left homeless, and with £40 in the world. She turned for help to either the Clergy Orphan Corporation or to the Sons of the Clergy, and I cannot now discover which, but it doesn't much matter. In your archives, there will be thousands of similar cases of need.

In those harsh days, a suicide was allowed no proper burial, no marked grave or memorial. 'I cannot conceive of a clergyman', said the coroner at the inquest, 'desecrating holy ground, as Mr Mayne has done, unless his mind was very much deranged.' His ashes were scattered to the four winds, and no one ever spoke of my father again. When I was fifteen, I was told the brief facts, but nothing more. What he was like, this unhappy man whose genes I carry, or what deep unhappiness led him to take such a desperate action, I could only guess. In the words of a friend of mine who was ten when his father took his own life:

> The sadness is you have lost a father you have never fully found. It's like a tune that ends before you have heard it out. Your whole life through you search to catch the strain, and seek the face you have lost in strangers' faces.

So that was that – until last year. For sometimes life comes full circle in the strangest, least predictable of ways, and there is a kind of healing.

Eighteen months ago, a letter arrived from the present rector saying that a few people in my father's village still remember what, for teenagers, had been a traumatic event in their lives, and would like to see a simple memorial stone placed in his church. I was moved by the offer, and we asked a good friend, a fine Irish sculptor, to carve a stone with his name and dates.

And then, one hot Sunday last August, on my mother's ninety-fourth birthday, we brought her back to the village with her grandchildren and great-grandchildren; at the morning Eucharist, the stone was dedicated; and I stood in my father's pulpit 60 years on and tried to find the right words to tell the father I had never really known – what? That I forgave him? That all was well? Yes, that certainly, but other things too.

I knew, as I stood in his pulpit, that I was not in some way claiming to atone by my own priesthood for my father's destructive act. We are each our own unique and responsible selves and answer to God for our own actions. But I am bone of his bone and flesh of his flesh, and there is that of my father in me which helps to make me what I am and which made it right to stand where he stood. I needed to say 'It's good to be back', for, although I knew it for so little time, the place where you are born and where you first learn to respond to the wonder and beauty of the world is in a very real sense home.

I needed to say: Only at a surface level is life merely a chronological sequence of events. There are certain happenings – the sudden loss of a parent in childhood, the death of a child, the breakdown of a marriage – that, because they are so traumatic and life-changing, seem to exist in a different dimension of time and be always part of you. Yet what really matters is not what happens in this unpredictable world, but *how* we respond, what we make of what we are given. Whether we have learned something about how even tragedy can be a means of grace that we might never have come to in any other way.

One of the deepest of all Christian insights is that even in the worst of events God is present and there are possibilities of redemption. That is part of the meaning of the Cross: that good can be brought out of evil; that new life can emerge from an event that seems utterly final and devastating. And I believe that we and the local body of Christ that is now my father's parish were saying to him:

> We shall never know *why* you did what you did, for that is known only to you and to God, but your desperate cry for help came out of so much unrecognized anguish of spirit that it demands not our judgement but our deep compassion.

So I needed also to say: One thing your action has taught me is that none of us really understands the heart of another human being, and none of us dares pass judgement on the life or death of another. That is God's prerogative, for he alone perfectly understands, and his judgement is always more than matched by his mercy. Those rare photographs I sometimes glance at merely catch the surface likeness: they tell us nothing of the secrets of the heart. Besides, those who find life too painful or too complex to bear may have the dice loaded against them from the start, and none of us knows whether we would survive if we had been in their place.

What we do know is that the God who is our judge is also our saviour, and that in Jesus Christ all we need to know of God is once and for all defined, defined in the only terms we can understand, in terms of a man who loves the sinner and heals the sick, who waits on those he calls his friends and washes their feet, who seeks out and consoles the despairing, who describes God as like a father waiting and watching for his penitent child to come home and who hangs on the Cross out of love for us.

The friend of whom I spoke just now has written this of his own father's death.

> God is present in such events not as their cause but as the one who even in the hardest of them offers us the possibility of that new life and healing which I believe is what salvation is . . . I cannot tell how God was present in my father's death . . . but my faith and my prayer is that

he was and continues to be present with him in ways beyond my guessing.

The possibility of new life, the certainty of healing, the power of 'the love that will not let me go', our eyes fixed not on the things that are seen but on the things that are unseen, 'for' (as St Paul writes) 'what is seen is transient, what is unseen is eternal'.

'No wonder we do not lose heart.' The God revealed by Christ is not only our creator who knows our inmost hearts but also our redeemer who, even as we turn to him in penitence, has forgiven us and welcomed us home. I do not believe my father needed me to tell him that, for I believe that when he fell to his death he was in the deepest sense caught and held in the everlasting arms of the one who is the merciful and loving Father of us all.

15. THE TENTH ANNIVERSARY OF THE CONSECRATION OF COVENTRY CATHEDRAL

(A sermon preached by The Very Revd Dr Edward H. Patey, Dean of Liverpool, 1964–82, in Coventry Cathedral on Sunday, 28 May 1972, on the occasion of the tenth anniversary of the consecration)

A few months ago, the magazine *Penthouse* had a cartoon in which two clergymen were shown looking at the unfinished west front of Liverpool Cathedral. One of them – possibly the Dean – is saying to the other 'To be honest, we're a little worried as to which will be finished first – the Cathedral or organised religion'.

That is fair comment, for it is a curious fact that whilst this is, undoubtedly, an age of cathedral building – Guildford, Coventry and two in Liverpool, it is also an age that has seen a dramatic decline in the influence and importance of institutional religion. Like many other people, I was sickened by the failure of the General Synod of the Church of England to take the seemingly elementary step of embarking on the first stage of unity with the Methodists, from whom we should never have been separated in the first place. But nobody can pretend any longer that the uniting (or failure to unite) of two ecclesiastical bodies will really make the slightest difference to the vast majority of men and women in this country. The goings-on in the churches seem to most people to have little relevance to the problems and opportunities of life, as they have to face them day by day.

So here is one of the strange paradoxes of the twentieth century. On the one hand, there has been great activity as new cathedrals are launched and old ones rescued (at great expense) from decay. On the other hand, the institution of religion, which cathedrals (more than any other kind of building) would seem to uphold, is clearly making less and less impact on the life of the nation and the individuals who make up that nation.

All of which would be rather depressing if it were not for a further fact, and one which sheds an entirely new light on the scene. For alongside the seemingly declining influence of the ecclesiastical set-up, there are clear signs all around that God is very far from dead. Here and there, often in the most unexpected places, we get hints of a spiritual awakening. It seems as if God is remaining faithful to his promise that death will be followed by resurrection, that out of the ruins of decaying and tired patterns of church life the gospel of Jesus will continue to rise, full of the promise of hope and victory.

A few swallows do not make a summer, so it would be premature to talk confidently about a religious revival. But there are enough signs on the horizon to kindle hope, and it has been the particular privilege of Coventry Cathedral in the first ten years of its life to reflect, within one place and through one ministry, many of those tokens of the renewal of the church which are beginning to give encouragement to Christian men and women the world over. It is not for Coventry to make any unique or special claim in this matter. I doubt whether anything has been discovered here these last ten years which has not been discovered elsewhere. But one thing is certain: the pattern of renewal has been focused in this place with a clarity and an intensity which has given Coventry in its first ten years of history a place of unique influence among the English cathedrals of our time.

What, then, are the particular things which have been discovered and proclaimed here these last ten years?

First – and it seems almost too obvious to say it – that in the proclamation of the gospel people matter more than anything else, and certainly more than buildings and struc-tures and traditions. This is obvious enough. Yet we easily become slaves to the plant and machinery of church life, easily become fossilized in stone and stained glass, in liturgy, music and ceremonial. Coventry began by being a fascinating experiment in church architecture, and it remains so. Yet the cathedral's greatest impact has turned out to be not primarily in terms of architecture but in terms of ministry and mission. People come here to see the cathedral only to discover that what matters even more than the building itself is what happens in the name of Christ within it and around it and because of it. In fact, the building of Coventry Cathedral may well turn out to have been one of the most important milestones in that necessary journey which the whole church must take as it moves away from the restrictions of institutionalism to the freedom of a dynamic movement.

It is a strange irony that these new discoveries about the unimportance of buildings have been made in the very places where the great twentieth-century cathedrals have been built – in Coventry, in Liverpool and in Washington.

The second discovery is that the Christian gospel can only come alive within the context of community. There is nothing new in this; indeed, it is at the heart of the Bible story. Further, it has been remarkably rediscovered in recent years at Iona, Taizé and Lee Abbey, and by the Focolari and the Jesus People. But Coventry was given the rare opportunity of assembling a team of ministers, clerical and lay, and creating a lively congregation, before the building itself had been completed. And even before the consecration ten years ago, as ministers and people were beginning to discover what it meant to be members one of another, the absolute necessity was being borne down upon them that somehow or other this sense of belonging to Christ and to one another must be brought to bear in the most practical ways upon the commercial, political, industrial, social and cultural life of the city, and eventually in a whole number of places on the international scene as well. It became obvious, too, that the Eucharist must be central to all this because it gives a kind of glimpse of what true community is meant to be. And to do this, the Eucharist had to evolve in such a way that the division between priests and people could be broken down until (though we have not yet reached this) we come to recognize that we are all equal partners in the celebration of the divine mysteries, albeit with different (and perhaps inter-changeable) jobs to do.

Again, it is strange that this discovery of the missionary power of community should have been made in a cathedral, for the Barchester image of cathedral life dies hard, with canons in residence treating each other with suspicion in the spirit of rivalry rather than community.

A third discovery is that our understanding of both evangelism and worship has been seriously clouded by our acceptance of the traditional, though wholly un-biblical belief that human experience can be divided neatly into two parts, the secular and the sacred. It is nearly a century since Bishop Westcott said that there was nothing secular except what is sinful, but we have taken a long time to learn this lesson. The Festival Service of the Arts, with the superb dance sequence choreographed by Dame Ninette de Valois, set the tone here early in the cathedral's life. A little later, Duke Ellington came here with his band. Since then, we have had the Bee Gees in Liverpool Cathedral, the Quintessence in Norwich Cathedral and the cast of *Hair* in St Paul's Cathedral. William Booth was re-echoing Martin Luther when he said that he did not see why the Devil should have all the best tunes. And the magnificent musical *Godspell*, now playing to capacity houses in the West End, seems the logical outcome of all this. Yet this is only a beginning. The discoveries that have to be made about God in the secular go far beyond the realms of music and dance and popular drama. Only when we can so involve ourselves in politics, in industry, in society, in education, in art and culture, and find ourselves able to dispense with church talk, Bible talk, and even God talk, and yet remain firmly theological, remain unmistakably Christian – only then will we be on the edge of discovering the real mystery of the Word of God made flesh.

Finally, Coventry, because of the very newness both of its architecture and its style of life, has helped us to recapture that vision of the essential flexibility of the pilgrim people of God, the people who must always be on the move. The extraordinary transformation from the few dozen loyal people who came to worship Sunday by Sunday with extreme discomfort in the underground crypt in the ruins in the mid-1950s to the queues and the crowds and the four-star tourist rating of the mid-1960s left those who were closely in touch with the cathedral at that time in no doubt at all that circumstances, or the Holy Spirit (or both), were hurrying us along at a breakneck speed. Here was an experience of almost Pentecostal dimension, and it put fresh hope into the hearts of millions who were beginning to wonder whether the church would ever again wake out of its slumbers. Today, this spiritual exhilaration is being experienced by Christians the world over, and often where you would least expect to find it.

But it is just here that a tenth-birthday celebration sounds a warning note, for even the most dynamic organism can be overtaken by the paralysis of institutionalism. How easily the spontaneity of Pentecost can turn into the 'Salisbury Use', or the 'Liverpool Use', or even 'what we always do here in Coventry'. Tradition is useful only if it remains a servant. But tradition likes to take over and become Boss, if it is given half a chance. This spells death, and sometimes we in the church seem to prefer the sleep of death to the alarming trumpet call to resurrection and new life.

The Resurrection of Jesus assures us that our Christian faith has an absolute, unconquerable permanence. But nothing else is permanent – not the way we express our faith nor the way we witness to it, nor the way we worship. And certainly there is nothing permanent about the form and structure of the church, which is bound to change from one generation to another.

In the early days of Coventry Cathedral, we felt ourselves very much to be 'starting from scratch'. Everything was an adventure into the unknown. There was nobody who could say 'you cannot do this for we have never done it'.

This gave us, as our faith in Jesus must always give us, a glimpse of that Heaven in which 'all things are made new'.

16. THE FIFTIETH ANNIVERSARY OF THE END OF WORLD WAR TWO

(A sermon preached on 6 August 1995 by The Very Revd Charles E. Kiblinger in St John's Cathedral, Denver, Colorado, at a service in remembrance of the end of World War Two. Dean Kiblinger has been Dean of St John's Cathedral since 1991)

It was November 1990 and I sat in the chancel of Coventry Cathedral, England, for the fiftieth anniversary of the bombing of that city and cathedral, the bombing in which the German Luftwaffe showed its muscle so frighteningly that the word *coventrate* came into the English language with its meaning 'to destroy utterly'. Beethoven's 'Moonlight' sonata had been played on BBC radio that night in 1940 to warn the citizens that the bombers were coming. As I sat there in 1990, I was aware that the 'Moonlight' sonata, being played from the back of the nave, was the first public performance of that sonata in that city for fifty years. As it was played, 1,075 autumn leaves fell from the soaring ceiling of the modern cathedral. They splashed down on the great stone altar where Mass was celebrated each Sunday. I looked back through the great three-storey glass wall out onto the ruins of the old bombed cathedral, its shell illuminated against the night sky, and I remembered the story of how the Provost of Coventry Cathedral had stood in those ruins on the morning after the bombing and said to the world over the BBC radio 'We will not respond in hatred and revenge but in forgiveness and reconciliation'.

It was not long afterwards that I stood in Dresden, Germany, in the cemetery where the charred remains of 100,000 victims of the bombing of that city are said to be buried. It was the annual observance of the date of that bombing, when the Allied bombers came and built their fires around the city, and the people, who thought the war was over, were coming out of hiding and going to the opera and filling up the streets. And the fires started and swept into the centre of the city with such rage that no one escaped.

We stood there in that cemetery, Germans, English and Americans, and sang in Latin 'dona nobis pacem' – 'give us peace' – and, as I stood next to the current Provost of Coventry Cathedral, I could hear the words of the old Provost of 1940, when he said 'We will respond not in hatred and revenge but in forgiveness and reconciliation'. It must have been a transfiguring experience for those who stood by the Provost and those prophetic words that called forth great disdain from many who heard them on the radio. They would go on for five years of one horror after another, working toward the end of the war, remembering somewhere within themselves that, no matter how much power was released, when it was all over, if it would ever be, it would be only the words of the old Provost that would bring healing, 'forgiveness and reconciliation', not 'hatred and revenge'. And little did they know that even if the war ended, which of course it inevitably did, there would follow 40 more years of cold war that lay under nuclear threat because those words were so impossible to hear. There would still be hatred and revenge loose in a world that could create fire-storms and atomic explosions which would have the power to destroy the whole planet. But as I stood there in the snow, where below our feet reverberated the memory of the awful power of the fire-storm, as I stood there with my German friends and British friends, I knew that the only thing that had the real power to transfigure this world were those words of the 1940s Provost: 'forgiveness and reconciliation' not 'hatred and revenge'.

And so I stand here in 1995, in this cathedral where Paul Roberts, one of its great deans, preached and presided through the years of World War Two as a pacifist, believing that in the end, when hell had had its way, the only thing that would transfigure this world was forgiveness and reconciliation. We come here remembering those fire-storms, a

Coventry and a Dresden, a London and a Hiroshima, a Pearl Harbor and a Nagasaki. We remember these past 40 years, when the power of nuclear war was held over our heads, and, even now, as the apparatus of cold war is disassembled, the nuclear threat is perpetuated by greedy hands that would profit from its sale to tiny nations where hatred and revenge could unleash unimaginable havoc upon this tiny globe.

In the gospel lesson for tonight, we have the transfiguration of Jesus whereby he is dramatically transfigured for the death he is to die in order to initiate a process of reconciliation between God and all creation. It is a radical, new thing; the prophets of old, Elijah and Moses, disappear at the end of the vision; and he is left alone to do a new thing. But what we didn't read tonight is what follows the vision, when he comes off the mountain. Once down to earth, where life goes on, he confronts the demonic – an evil spirit is to be cast out.

Much of what war has been about in all its many forms and in its limited and unlimited forms has been about the projection of the demonic upon another. Who is the enemy? How many times have I heard discussion of international discord and threats against our nation when someone said 'Nuke 'em!' When I hear that, when I get in touch with the hatred and revenge in my own heart and when I get caught up in the mass hatred and revenge with its racist, sexist, nationalist and economic phobic overtones, I know that if we would be transfigured it will only come through forgiveness and reconciliation. I know that Jesus' way, the new order he initiates as he comes off the mount and heads for Jerusalem where hatred and revenge will have its way with him, the way of forgiveness and reconciliation that is declared in his death and Resurrection, will be all that will save us. And furthermore, when I get in touch with the hatred and revenge in me and my brothers and sisters and in the politics of a Bosnia Herzegovina or a Chechnya, I know that, if we continue to project the demonic beyond ourselves, hatred and revenge will continue to have its way with us, for we have met the enemy and it is not the Russians or the Japanese or the Germans or the nasty people who live across the street.

The enemy is us. When we begin the business of forgiveness and reconciliation at home in our hearts, in our families, in our churches and in our community then we will know that the new order that was initiated by Jesus on the mount of transfiguration will stop at nothing less than the whole earth.

And so we stand at the end of two wars, one full of fire and the other cold, still holding the power of the atom in our hands. And whatever we do with that power, it is still God's order and, in the transfigured Jesus, he has declared that the old order is passing away and a new order is upon us. It is now perhaps the moment in history when we have the greatest opportunity to join in the building of that new order. And if we would, it will be just like the old Provost said in those smouldering ruins of a world war, 'We will respond not with hatred and revenge but with forgiveness and reconciliation'.

17. CATHEDRALS, UNIVERSITIES AND PEACEMAKING

(A sermon preached before the University of Oxford on Remembrance Sunday, 12 November 1989, by The Very Revd Horace Dammers, Dean of Bristol, 1973–87)

Blessed are the peacemakers, for they shall be called sons of God.
MATTHEW 5.9

Today most if not all of us would wish to add 'and daughters' to this text in recognition of the vital role of women in the making of peace. Is not war 'detested by mothers', as the poet Horace observed? It is the peacemakers, as distinct from those who are merely peacelovers, whom Jesus calls blessed. It is not enough simply to desire peace. No, we are actively to pursue it. On this Remembrance Sunday, let us look together at our Christian calling to be makers of peace. I offer this sermon in memory of those who gave their lives in two world wars.

I shall share with you the stories of five modest efforts at peacemaking which were made at Bristol Cathedral when I was Dean there. Then I shall briefly offer you five ideas about the vocation to peacemaking of this university and its members. All the Bristol stories are of small-scale events. All were ecumenical. All except one were initiated by lay people. All involved potential or actual controversy and were therefore in some small sense costly.

The first story concerns a special service, something at which cathedrals hopefully excel. A substantial number of the unemployed, mainly young people, had organized a march from all over the country, converging on London to present their case to the government. In many cities *en route*, there were civic receptions, speeches of welcome and parades to mark their arrival. But in Bristol, Ron Nethercott, the regional secretary of the Transport and General Workers' Union, persuaded his colleagues to ask instead for a service at the cathedral. Our bishop broke his sabbatical to attend. The Salvation Army provided a band to complement the efforts of the Cathedral Choir, and an ecumenical service was carefully crafted to express the hope for a more just and peaceful society, in which the underprivileged, the unemployed in particular, would be liberated from their oppression. One local Member of Parliament attended, but another wrote to me to protest against the cathedral being involved in so political a matter. One young man told me afterwards over a cup of tea that, though he was himself an unbeliever, the service had been the greatest spiritual experience of his life.

My second story concerns the setting aside of a chapel in the cathedral for prayer for peace, again an initiative particularly appropriate for a cathedral, with its usually more than adequate space for new ventures and its central position in the life of the city or county. A small group of lay women and men, including Roman Catholics, Quakers, Methodists and Anglicans, called on me with a request that they might organize regular prayers for peace in the cathedral. It would have been a difficult request to refuse, even if I had been minded to do so. So we set aside a chapel, put up peace posters and lit a large candle daily for peace. Later, we installed a candlestand and invited people to light their own candles. We also associated the chapel with the work of Amnesty International. A monthly silent vigil for peace was established, and many visitors came to pray and record their visit in the visitors' book, Sikhs, Muslims, Hindus and Jews, as well as Christians. Even this supposedly innocent enterprise, however, did not escape criticism, as intemperate remarks in the visitors' book bore witness.

Later, a similar ecumenical group of lay people came to see me with a further request. After the Falklands War, they wished to take an initiative of reconciliation and collect money locally for the benefit of Argentinian war widows and orphans and war disabled. I was able to arrange for the Bristol Council of Christian Churches to provide them with banking and back-up facilities, and for the World Council of Churches to negotiate the transfer of funds to an appropriate and reliable Christian agency. They collected about £3,000. A reporter from a national daily phoned me for information about this transaction and gave me his unsolicited opinion that their action amounted to high treason.

My fourth story pleases me even more. At the height of their terrible war, a small group of Iranian and Iraqi residents in the Bristol area came to ask me to lead them in a prayer meeting in our Peace Chapel, prayer for peace between their two countries. In doing so, they were taking a risk, as it is unlikely that either of their governments would have approved of their action. It required careful thought to lead in prayer the small group of Christians and Muslims who assembled in our Peace Chapel, with a reporter from Radio Bristol in attendance with his tape recorder. After the service, we all walked to the City's war memorial, where the Iranians laid a wreath for the Iraqi dead and vice versa. In the light of the unpredictably sudden ending of that awful war, who can tell how the Holy Spirit may have used that beautiful action by a handful of brave young men and women?

My fifth and last story is the only one which was not initiated by lay people. One Remembrance-tide, I wrote an article in the *Church Times*, quoting Mountbatten, Eisenhower and others and proposing that those of us who had participated in war as combatants had both a right and a duty to be active in the cause of international peace and disarmament. If, for example, those of us who wished to do so were jointly to protest against the deployment of nuclear arms in our country, no one could accuse us war veterans of being unpatriotic or out of touch with reality, the usual sneers against active peacemakers.

As a consequence of this article, four of us, two Christians and two Jews, met in the Cathedral Refectory for lunch, and the Ex-Services Campaign for Nuclear Disarmament was born. This organization has more than fulfilled my hopes for it. However, I have found that the association of the church with the popular desire to rid ourselves of these genocidal weapons can engender violent and abusive opposition.

At a big conference of North American and British deans and provosts at Washington Cathedral some years ago, I was able briefly to introduce the idea of having a Peace Chapel in a cathedral. Later, at a conference of English deans and provosts in London, it was agreed that our secretary should write and commend the idea to cathedrals throughout the Anglican Communion. I was delighted, a few years later, to find such a chapel recently established as far away as Grafton Cathedral, New South Wales, and, more recently still, in Truro Cathedral.

Now, to what is for me the more difficult bit, the vocation to peacemaking of this great university and its members, more difficult because, from the most recent undergraduate to the most senior professor, each of you knows more about this university than I do. So what I have to say demands the closest critical scrutiny on your part to discern whether it mediates to you the word of God or not.

The first point presents the university as a temple of coherence. The very word 'university', like the word 'universe', by definition 'uni', one, 'versity', turning, implies a dynamic approach to the coherence of all experience, all knowledge, a coherence which is rooted in the unity of the One Creator God. It is essential to the inner vocation of a university to the reconciliation with one another of observed facts, of experiences and of people, a reconciliation which is closely related to peacemaking and, as I say, ultimately grounded in the unity of the Creator God.

The second, more down-to-earth point presents the university as a provider of learning opportunities. Within Western Europe, British universities have pioneered the establishment of academic disciplines in the fields of peacemaking and the resolution of conflict. I know of such enterprises in the universities of Bradford and of Kent, and there may well be others. I also know that there are influential people in this university who are personally interested in the establishment of a department of Peace Studies in the University of Cassino, southern Italy, a particularly appropriate venue for at least two reasons. Monte Cassino, of course, was the home of St Benedict whose followers have always been committed to the vocation of peacemaking. 'Pax in Spinis', peace among the thorns, is a Benedictine motto. The second reason is that Cassino was the scene of one of the toughest battles in World War Two. Over 20,000 bodies lie in the German War Cemetery there, a beautiful but hauntingly sad place. There are also Commonwealth, French and Italian War Cemeteries in the area and an American one not far away. I remember that the first time I visited the Commonwealth Cemetery, one of the first gravestones that I saw bore t45he name of a school friend of mine, a poignant moment that may be recalled in passing on this Remembrance Sunday.

The third point presents the university as a partner in the political process. In his book *Perestroika*, President Gorbachev had this to say about the contribution of scientists and scholars to the peacemaking process.

> Meetings with such people not only enrich one's theory and philosophy, but have also influenced the political moves and decisions that had to be taken in recent years. I well remember my meeting in November 1985 with a delegation from a Nobel Prize-Winners' congress . . . The scientists handed me an appeal from the participants in their congress and we had a very serious discussion about the possible consequences of the use of nuclear weapons, the importance of banning nuclear tests and the dangers of militarising space. We agreed that efforts for security through disarmament should be combined with efforts to guarantee man decent conditions of existence.

My next point concerns the university's role as an exemplary community. As peacemakers, you are personally called to protest against the snide remark about a colleague, which poses as wit, and to reconcile relationships that are potentially or actually hostile. As peacemakers within the university, you are to be kindly and generous in your appreciation of the talents and personalities of others. As peacemakers, too, you can help to ensure that domestic and other non-academic staff are treated with respect and enjoy appropriate conditions of work and pay. No doubt other ways will occur to you in which you can do your bit to ensure that university and college life are exemplary in terms of justice and peace.

Finally, I present this ancient university as sustainer of personal vocation. University sermons are no longer popular occasions, unless possibly a nationally known name is announced as preacher. By your presence here this Remembrance-tide, you have selected yourselves for the personal vocation of peacemaking. You are all very special people in terms of God's will for true peace in his world. I invite you, therefore, to ponder and pray about your personal vocation to peacemaking in your home, at your work, in your local church, in the world at large. Blessed are you, each one of you, peacemakers, for you shall be called the sons and daughters of God.

18. CHRISTMAS EVE

(A sermon for Christmas Eve 1993 preached in Bristol Cathedral by The Very Revd Dr Wesley Carr, Dean of Bristol, 1987–97, Dean of Westminster, 1997–)

The Word was made flesh
JOHN 1.14

Christmas was once abolished in this country. After the execution of King Charles I the Puritans thought it frivolous and excessive. In the past few weeks we may sometimes have felt they had a point. But not tonight, with its sense of eternity in a moment. They did not just stop the eating, drinking and dancing. On Christmas Day 1657, John Evelyn went to church to receive communion, just as we do tonight. The chapel was surrounded by soldiers,

> men of high flight [he wrote] and above ordinances, who spake spiteful things of our Lord's nativity; as we went up to receive the sacrament, the miscreants held their muskets against us as if they would have shot us at the altar.

In the end, the Puritans did not manage to abolish Christmas. They were wrong to try and probably had no chance. But on one point they were right: they realized that you cannot separate the festivity from the worship, the pagan side from the Christian, or the worldly from the religious. Christmas is both or neither. Amid the razzmatazz of human life, Christ is born: 'The Word was made *flesh* and dwelt among *us*.'

What is this 'Word'? When we speak, we express who we are and what we mean to do. So the Word stands for being and action. In the moment of the Word made flesh God

79

states who he is and what he does. Tonight, we are not celebrating a world being magically altered once and for all, but we confess that even now there is still hope for our old, familiar world. The Christmas story is not a series of improbable miracles: this night of nights, in this moment's worship, we celebrate God's eternal trust in us.

That's why the old stories remain enthralling: the manger is the throne of heaven – eternity in a moment; the shepherds, irreligious men and social outcasts, are the first to worship – eternity in the unlikely; wise men from afar, alien pilgrims, find their goal – eternity now for everyone, with no exceptions. But all of them experience only a moment. They cannot stay; each has to go back to their old lives; Mary and Joseph return to Nazareth; the shepherds return to their flocks; the wise men escape Herod and go home by a different route. As Edwin Muir, in his remarkable poem 'The Transfiguration', poignantly puts it:

> Reality or vision, this we have seen.
> If it had lasted but another moment
> It might have held for ever! But the world
> Rolled back into its place, and we are here,
> And all that radiant kingdom lies forlorn

'And we are here.' In the Christmas carnival, we cannot ignore the grimness of things. Had I a thousand hours, I could not tonight in the name of God offer a solution to the world's appalling dilemmas – atrocities in Bosnia or Ireland, murder and rape, child abuse, fraud and deceit and all our wickedness. In all of these (and many more), we face those human and ruinous blemishes that are each of us – the flesh. But they are eternally part of Christmas, too. 'The Word was made flesh' – God is caught up in all our life, even its most appalling parts.

But because God is with us he is truly 'Saviour'. He is *with* us, and he rescues us from captivity to our imperfection. The evils of our world do not vanish because of Christmas. We might wish it, but none of us is foolish enough to believe that. Those notorious and destructive failings that we see so quickly in others we each know in ourselves. But because the Word is made flesh these no longer need destroy. God can turn the old and all too familiar vices into creative moments of eternity.

In Christ, pride – our self-regarding selves – becomes neighbour-serving humility; in Christ, covetous desire to own becomes generosity; in Christ, lust, our eagerness to possess, yields to self-giving love; in Christ, the insidious destructiveness of envy gives way to admiration of the other person; in Christ, the excess of gluttony is transformed into restraint that leads to concern for all in need; in Christ, anger feeds a longing for justice, not for judgement alone; and above all in Christ, despairing old sloth, the chief vice of our age, our bored disenchantment with everything, becomes that lively amazement which is worship.

So what of ourselves? All the things which destroy human life do not vanish in the romance of tonight. They remain what they are – human nature, the flesh. But now we celebrate this: the flesh is where God is already. Because the Word became flesh, what is basically us can become in moments and actions divine. When such eternity is disclosed, we cannot stand and watch: we must worship and adore. As we can, we make the truth our own.

The longest journey starts with a single step. On the first Christmas night, Mary and Joseph, the shepherds and the magi, the angels and the Son of God himself, each took their one step which forever changed the world. Tonight, eternity is again disclosed when we each pray for Christ to be born in us, return to our everyday lives and act in that faith. Here is the eternal mystery and practical truth of Christmas – the moment of Christ's birth in the manger at Bethlehem and the eternity of his birth tonight in our hearts.

19. EASTER DAY

(A sermon for Easter Day, 1983, preached in Durham Cathedral by The Very Revd Dr Peter Baelz, Dean of Durham, 1980–88)

You shall draw water with joy from the springs of deliverance.
ISAIAH 12.3

An encouraging and typically Easter thought. But what am I to do if, when I sit back and think more deeply, I find Good Friday unbearable and Easter unbelievable? Good Friday – the death of one who gave himself completely to the service of goodness, mercy and compassion. Obedience to God and love for his fellow men brings him in the end to a cross, then death and burial. Surely this is the final triumph of evil? Surely this reveals what we have long suspected in our hearts, that the whole of the human story is characterized by wickedness and stupidity rather than by goodness and wisdom? And surely when we reflect, we see the Cross as but one episode in a long chapter of such events – Auschwitz, Cambodia, violence in almost every country we can imagine, conflict and destruction – and human history, far from being the triumph of witness and wisdom which we like to believe, is really in the long run a tale told by an idiot, signifying nothing? How could our full gaze on the Cross and upon its significance be anything else than unbearable, because it exposes our most sensitive nerve, and we know within ourselves that, even if we are not, you and I, desperately wicked, we are weak and flawed, battered about by forces over which we seem to have no power, taking us we know not where? Good Friday, *Good* Friday! Good Friday, unbearable Friday. But, you may say, we must see alongside Good Friday, Easter. I agree. But what if I said that, when I reflect, I find not only

Good Friday unbearable but also Easter unbelievable? Is this not one more human device to ease the burden of this intolerable world, to imagine that after death there is a better world, a better life, something which we can look forward to which will make all things different? Is this not that very kind of opium or drug which perhaps alone for many of us (and, God knows, let us not judge ourselves on this too harshly) makes life tolerable? But when I reflect and use my reason, I have been taught to distrust stories of the supernatural. And Easter is supernatural, whatever else it is. I have been taught to think twice when I hear about 'ghoulies, ghosties and long-leggity beasties and things that go bump in the night'. I have been taught to see that the world, the natural world, is much more complex, much more mysterious perhaps, than we imagined, and that human beings make up stories, they create images, they live off their imaginations. But the world, the natural world, goes its own way. So when I hear of stories including empty tombs, visionary experiences, what am I to make of it? Can these really be proofs that Good Friday is not the whole story? Surely there are no proofs. 'All proofs or disproofs that we tender of God's existence are returned unopened to the sender.' When I reflect in this way on the unbearableness of Good Friday and the incredibility of Easter, I am doing no more than exercising my God-given human mind. You may say 'Well, this is just what you have got to drop on this occasion. There is no way by thought. You have simply to believe.' But can we really believe simply, without having at least some idea of the rhyme and reason, the pattern, of what we are believing?

I suggest that from the human angle Good Friday is unbearable and Easter is frankly incredible. But maybe, just maybe, our human minds do not see the whole of the story. What they see may be true and important, and our human minds are God's gift which prevents us from just dreaming things up, putting our faith in dreams. We need reality, not dreams, if we are ever going to make this world a place more like God's kingdom. But supposing it is not the whole thing that we see. Supposing there is more to it. Supposing there is, if you like, given to us, momentarily, God's side of the story. Supposing he has shown men and women here and there, witnesses of the Resurrection, his saints, his people, a different side both of Good Friday and Easter. What could this be?

Well, first let Easter throw its light on Good Friday, because whatever Easter may be, whatever that cluster of events and experiences may have been, one result of Easter was a new look at Good Friday. And that new look presented something astonishing. No longer simply dereliction, no longer simply death and despair, but rather the divine love. How could this be? A death the divine love? And yet this is what the early Christians proclaimed, that God commended his love towards us in that, while we were yet sinners, Christ died for us. The early Christians had their own problems how to make this plain, how to spell it out, how to communicate their faith. They did so in a variety of ways. But one way, which I think still has something to say to us, is this: that Good Friday is God's love giving itself to his creation, his wayward, wicked, stupid creation, giving itself to his creation to the full. God pours himself out into his world as man, to share man's condition. That is the measure of his love. And so what we see as man's breaking, for such the Cross is, is also God's making, because it signifies to us the extent, the depth, the height of his love. He will not let us go. He is there in the darkest place. In death and hell itself and in bitter agony he is there before us. When we human beings find ourselves in similar places we know we are not alone.

If the life given on the Cross is God's life, then perhaps Easter itself may begin to make sense. Perhaps Good Friday can throw light on Easter. Perhaps on Easter we ought to have a sermon about Good Friday, and on Good Friday the sermon about Easter, because the two are one. If on the Cross it is *God's* life, giving itself utterly, knowing what it means to be God-forsaken, to be one among sinners, to be derelict and alone, to cry out as if there is no God, if that is the measure of God's love and if that is invincible, if it cannot be overcome because it is *God's* love, then perhaps Easter, in God's way of seeing things, follows naturally. God has taken into himself his creature's, his nature's, his human nature's full godlessness and despair, but his love remains unbroken. Our loves go a little way from time to time, but in the end they all break. But God's love, that is unbreakable.

So perhaps, if we may speak in picture language, the story from God's side is not letting things get absolutely bad and then suddenly waking up and reversing them all and making them good again. It is rather giving of self and love to the world, to his world, to the full. And the pattern remains the same. It is the *giving* of his life and, in so giving, giving *life*. Perhaps dare we hope today, and draw joy from the springs of deliverance, from the faith that God's love is invincible, and that what is supernatural about Easter is in the end the grace of God, that he gives to us an experience, a faith, an inkling, that love, his love, will, and does triumph? I think we know from time to time that this is so, that love, taken to the end, seeming to be broken, finds its way to new life again and is remade, that the way to life is the way of love that is of self-giving and of dying to self. Therefore, perhaps we can have reason, divine reason, to proclaim today our faith in the risen Christ, as one who gives himself still to us, not only in his historical times but also today, through one another, through his word, through sacrament, through the loving actions of men and women. There is our joy. The deliverance which comes to us from beyond ourselves, that is the true supernatural, so super that we may not notice its presence among us. This is our Easter message, our Easter joy, our Easter hope. Then we dare follow in the steps which Christ himself taught us, we dare perhaps walk, haltingly, hopefully, the way of love, the way of sacrifice, the way of justice and mercy. This is what we are called to – that we walk that way. Then perhaps we shall know in our own hearts that Jesus Christ lives, because the one who collected a band of disciples around him continues to do so, to give them life that they may give life to others.

20. CAIN AND ABEL

(A sermon on Cain and Abel preached by The Very Revd Dr John Drury, Dean of Christ Church, Oxford, 1991–)

The story of Cain and Abel has tragic power: the first murder motivated by that sibling jealousy which is known in every family of more than three, with its accompanying and bitter complaints of unfairness.

It presupposes the mysterious and universal institution of sacrifice. It does not explain it, though it lies very near its dark heart. Cain the farmer sacrificed his corn, Abel the shepherd 'the firstlings of his flock'. Professor Walter Burkert's theory about sacrifice is the best on offer. It runs as follows. Before people were either farmers or shepherds they were hunters, killing to eat. This was a much more dangerous livelihood, always under the fear of violent death: the horror of the death of the prey, the possibility of the prey killing the hunter, or one hunter accidentally killing another, the possibility of there being no more animals to kill. Sacrifice, says Burkert, controlled these terrors by containing them within the predictable order of ritual which secured the approval of God and brought the community together. The animal was set apart and purified, and the moment of its death was followed by a common meal of its meat in which God and community participated in *koinonia* or communion.

This ancient and terrible performance hovers in the background of our customary service this morning. It is terrible because of what it tells us about ourselves. We proudly call ourselves *homo sapiens*, intelligent man. Burkert's researches have led him to call us *homo necans*, killer man. Both apply to our own century, with the huge achievement of our sciences and the hecatombs, the millions, of slain humanity. And here we remember just one victim of long ago, a heretic crucified

86

in the interests of political and religious order. Do we do well to set such victimization amid the upholstered comforts of liturgy, following the lead of our killer ancestors?

Sacrifice has always had its critics and, according to the Bible, the foremost among them is God:

> What to me is the multitude of your sacrifices? says the
> Lord;
> I have had enough of burnt offerings of rams and the fat
> of fed beasts;
> I do not delight in the blood of bulls, or of lambs, or of
> he-goats.
>
> . . . even though you make many prayers, I will not listen;
> your hands are full of blood.
>
> . . . remove the evil of your doings from before my eyes;
> cease to do evil, learn to do good;
> seek justice, correct oppression; . . .
>
> Isaiah 1.11, 15b, 16b–17a

So in our story. God respected Abel's sacrifice but not Cain's. Judging by God's surprise at Cain's fierce resentment of this apparent unfairness, it is not an important matter as far as he is concerned. He prefers mutton to muesli today. So what? It is moral deeds that matter.

> If thou doest well, shalt thou not be accepted?

And God knows that doing well is a constant effort of resisting evil. Let it slip for a moment and

> sin coucheth at the door; its desire is for you, but you
> must master it.

He leaves Cain, as he leaves us, to get on with it. But Cain's world has been toppled out of control by God's airy liturgical negligence. As a medicine for his disordered feelings he prefers the fierce, exhilarating indulgence of anger to the patient self-control of doing the good he can. He walks his brother out into the fields and kills him there. God turns up again and notices, surprised again, that someone – one of the four humans on earth – is missing:

Where is Abel thy brother?

and Cain answers:

I know not. Am I my brother's keeper?

That sour reply has become a commonplace, so readily does it come to our minds if not our lips as we, or our elected politicians, brush aside the victims of our hatreds, fears and negligences. But to God it is an appalling evasion, winding his surprise up to a higher pitch than before, even a wailing lament:

What hast thou done? The voice of thy brother's blood crieth unto me from the ground.

He sends Cain off to be a fugitive and a vagabond. Yet his patience with the humanity whom he made to be of one blood and communion is not exhausted. As with his parents, he will protect Cain in his exile, marking him so that he will not, in his turn, be killed but may learn 'to bear the beams of love' (Blake) and control his lethal instincts.

And that is the work and business of our lives too. The haunting image of sin couching at the door, longing to get at us as soon as we lift the latch, while we must resist it and rule over it – that describes our constant condition. We are always among what the sombre hymn calls 'the manifold temptations that death alone can cure'. The dark side of sacrifice, the isolation and killing of the victim, confronts us in this service with something dreadfully real in our human nature. It can bring with it the astringent gift of penitence, that very valuable part of our liturgy. It is the first and necessary step in resisting evil. We acknowledge the truth of our participation in the works of darkness.

Then, in the order of our service, we are made to realize that that does not exhaust the truth of our condition. There is goodness available to us, and a goodness in us that wants it and can take it. That goodness comes by way of Christ. As the writer of the Epistle to the Hebrews says mysteriously, his blood 'speaks better things than the blood of Abel'. How so? He suffered Abel's fate and the fate of the firstlings of Abel's flock, which is why we call him the lamb. But this time it is different.

Firstly, it is not some other that is seized upon as the victim, whether lamb or human brother. It is the self – 'the one oblation of himself once offered' – which is laid hold upon, given away for the others who happen to be around, and proves to be really effective for good – as rituals can never be. 'Take, eat, this is my body which is given for you . . . this is my blood which is shed for you for the remission of sins.'

Secondly, Christ makes amends for the divine negligence in the ancient story. Cain's offering of 'the fruit of the ground' is respected and set to perpetual use. Bread and wine become the Christian common meal for ever after, and the means of achieving the society, conviviality or communion which was the aim and object of sacrifice all along.

So finally, at this point a later episode in the biblical legend of Cain comes to mind. He built the first city. So he got there in the end, for the social cohesion which the city represents is the end and goal of sacrifice, healing the lethal wound and bringing social life. And the builder of a city is, as the ancients knew very well, a kind of super-shepherd, bringing humanity into the safety of a fold. So Cain took up his brother's work and took it further.

These things are mysteries which symbols and legends show and hide. We can only guess their meanings. But what we all know is that we are summoned to the negative endurance of resisting evil, and also to positive works of charity: feeding our neighbours and strengthening the wise and compassionate bonds of society. Or, as our prayer puts it, to 'continue in that holy fellowship and do all such good works as thou hast prepared for us to walk in'.

21. JACOB AND THE ANGEL

(A sermon by The Very Revd Charles E. Kiblinger in St John's Cathedral, Denver, Colorado)

Propers: Genesis 32.22–31;
Romans 9.1–5; Matthew 14.13–21

'The sun rose upon him as he passed Penuel, limping because of his hip.' If Jacob limped the rest of his life, it must have been a great blow to an egotistical go-getter like him. After all, he was the one who had inherited the wealth of the family, dreamed dreams about being the father of a great nation and, despite the trick his uncle Laban played on him by giving him his plain daughter instead of the beautiful one, in the end Jacob got the beautiful one as well and managed to trick Laban into sending him off with a good piece of *his* wealth too.

Jacob was an overachiever. It was said that even in the womb he wrestled with his twin brother Esau. Jacob was born competing to be the best, even though Esau succeeded in being the first-born. Jacob was bent on being a winner at all costs. So he tricked his trusting brother into giving him the older child's inheritance, cheated his father out of his blessing by taking advantage of him in the weakness of his old age and then, instead of facing up to what he had done, he took off for Laban's country, for fear of the wrath of Esau. If Jacob ended up limping the rest of his life, it must have been a low blow to the man who always had to be lookin' good.

And then there was the long night on the river bank. He was on his way home with his wives and children and new-found wealth. He had prayed to God to protect him and his family from Esau's wrath, and just to cover his bet he had sent ahead an impressive collection of fine gifts to sweeten the meeting with his hairy old twin brother. Everyone crossed the river but him. He stayed on the other side, alone in the dark.

That's where we pick up the story in our first lesson for today. And the story goes that he wrestled with God all night. That's where the limp comes from, because it says that God put his hip out of joint. But Jacob, true to form, was determined to win even a wrestling match with God and, even in his pain, would not let go until God gave him his blessing. But unlike the time he tricked his blind old father, he didn't get the blessing. Instead, God asks him for his name, and, in the ancient world, a name was not just a label. If you revealed your name to another, you revealed your character; and so, when the lame wrestler says 'Jacob', he reveals his character as a deceiver and a cheat – as the overachiever who has built the image of success at great cost to others, even those nearest and dearest, like brothers and fathers and uncles.

It is the moment of truth. In the night, alone, on the other side of the river from home, wrestling with God, the truth finally comes into consciousness. Its awful reality is played out in the imagination and, for once, the self reflected in the water is clear. There can be no coming home until there is a coming home to the true self. There can be no reconciliation until there is a reconciliation with the self. There can be no restitution until there is a restitution of the soul. Jacob, the achiever, the builder, the succeeder, the charmer, the handsome man of enduring youth and beauty, moves beyond image to inner truth. In the night of wrestling with God, God wrestles from him the truth, and deceit is converted to humble honesty. There is clear insight into the totality of the self in the full spectrum of its strengths and weaknesses. It is in the darkness of this soul-searching that the ever-confident winner faces failure as part of his life too.

And so God gives him a new name – Israel – it means the one who is willing to strive and struggle with God and man for, in his willingness to stay behind on the other side of the river in the darkness and struggle with truth, he has become whole.

It is at this point that Jacob is ready for God's blessing, not because he has achieved it but because he has become whole. He has recognized the whole truth about himself. He lives no longer in winner's denial but is open to the whole of himself – good, bad and in-between. Hence he is ready to be made holy.

But Jacob takes one step forward and two backwards. 'Please tell me your name', he says. He has walked through the valley of humility, but now he wants some control back. In the ancient world, to name the god or demon you confronted would mean you had the power to hold on to it, to summon it, obligate it. And so Jacob, ever wont to obligate, manipulate and control others for his own success, tries to grasp the holy for his own ends. And then God asks 'Why is it that you ask my name?' There is no answer. The question hangs provocatively in the air. And in the silence one can feel the sinking of the truth once more back into the heart of Jacob, the deceiver, now become Israel the struggler. It is then that God gives him his blessing. The man who had become whole was declared holy. He was declared holy not by his achievement but by his struggle with his own true self until he could discover that it was not a matter of winning love but of accepting it as a free gift despite himself.

'And the sun rose upon him as he passed Penuel, limping because of his hip.' And one can suppose that from time to time, when he had to limp across a room in front of a lot of people, he would be reminded of the night on the river bank where he found out who he really was and that he was loved anyway.

It's a story for all of us, this one. It is a story about each of us in our journey to an authentic relationship to God, ourselves and our world. It calls us to a humble and honest struggle with truth. And the struggle on the other side of the bank before we can come home to ourselves and those we love and the God who loves us, despite what we discover in the struggle, is probably a repeated experience in all of our lives as we seek to come to a place of wholeness.

But this saga in Genesis is not just about individuals. It is about a whole nation – Israel; it is about a nation that struggled with having to be always a winner; it is about a nation full of romantic idealism about itself that kept it in denial of its failures and weaknesses; and God was forever waking it up to the truth about itself.

Perhaps on this Sunday when we read the gospel story of the feeding of the five thousand, we are reminded of the flawed fabric of a rich society where we are all of us here the richest of people by world standards, yet live with those who don't have enough to eat, at our doorstep. As a nation, we are reminded by this story that our need to be winners may be keeping us from the truth of a have and have-not society. And maybe if we could begin to struggle with that and become honest about it we could reach for a new wholeness in which the truth of the feeding of the five thousand could become a reality. Maybe we could realize the message of this story, that there is indeed enough for everybody so that all might be filled.

'And the sun rose upon him as he passed Penuel, limping because of his hip.'

22. FAITH OUTSIDE THE CHURCH

(A sermon for a parish church in Norwich preached on Sunday, 22 September 1996, being the Sunday after the Celebration of the Eucharist in Norwich Cathedral on its 900th anniversary, by The Very Revd Dr Alan Webster, Dean of Norwich, 1970–78, and Dean of St Paul's, 1978–87)

Luke 7.1–10 from the Jerusalem Bible, the Gospel for Pentecost 17 in the ASB, 2nd year

The centurion, a senior officer in the Roman army in charge of 100 men, was vital to the whole structure of the Roman Empire. Centurions had to be skilled, confident, informed and courageous in order to hold together this huge international force which kept the peace in Europe, more or less, for 400 years. Our ancestors in this part of Britain were riotous, even more riotous than Tombland or King Street today on a Saturday night. To deal with the Iceni, centurions, both active and retired, were settled in Colchester to keep the peace; and, in the countryside, retired centurions often became farmers. We would say, in modern English, that they were the solid people in cities and in the countryside. There is evidence that centurions took an interest in the religious practices of the countries where they were stationed. (See C. F. Evans, *St Luke*, SCM, 1990, pp. 341–5.)

The centurion in St Luke's story had heard of the renowned local healer and prophet, Jesus Christ. St Luke emphasized the fact that he did not go to meet Christ, but sent messengers, sympathetic messengers, because though he would not have gone to a Jewish synagogue himself, he had been helpful in the building of a synagogue, rather as British administrators in the Sudan used to help Muslims to perform their religious duties. The centurion did not make any personal fuss. He assumed – and here we see his faith – that Christ, like him, could issue orders, and his 'beloved' servant (perhaps it means his 'invaluable' servant – the man who could manage the files, keep the communications open) could be healed by a message. It's as if we phoned the clinic; the secretary said 'The doctor will come this morning' and we said 'No, just fax me and I'll get the prescription sent up from the chemist'. The centurion in the story assumed that Christ had the same facilities that he had himself for getting things done.

We are told that Christ was astonished. He turned around and said rather solemnly to the crowd, so that they would really notice his words, 'I tell you, not even in Israel have I found faith like this'. This startling story is something for us to treasure in days when we are often discontented about ourselves as Christians, and about our church as an organization.

Yesterday, at the 900th anniversary celebrations of Norwich Cathedral, the Archbishop of Canterbury was talking about the sillinesses of the church, before he went on to be strongly encouraging. He quoted the traditional MP who said of the old 1662 Prayerbook 'It was good enough for St Paul, it's good enough for me', and the church noticeboard: 'Don't let worry kill you off: let the church help.' In today's Gospel, we are taught that Christ himself drew attention to God at work outside Israel.

When we are alert, we shall often find the Spirit coming to us from people right outside the church. An American bishop was driving home to Cape Cod after taking a five day retreat for the Sisters of St Margaret at Duxbury, near Boston, Massachusetts. He was feeling tired – even hungry. Five days' silence, and no one talking but himself. The food had been full of vitamins but, as he said in an old-fashioned American phrase, 'It did not stick to the stomach'. So he stopped near Hyannis to buy a coffee and a doughnut. He was leaning on his car in the sun when, to his astonishment, a huge truck drew up beside him. The truck driver leant out and shouted 'How's the doughnut, Father?' The startled bishop replied

'Excellent'. 'Good', said the truck driver, who started his vast vehicle and drove off, leaving the bishop delighted at the humour, the good nature. The bishop felt at one with life and at one with God. A truck driver from right outside the church had given him the encouragement, the faith, he needed. (See J. B. Coburn, *Grace in All Things*, Cowley, 1995.)

When we fasten on the verses in the Bible and in Christian worship about sin and guilt, and get obsessed with what's wrong with the church, we can forget that all the time God is at work outside the church. All the time, scientists are making astonishing discoveries which can beat back the frontiers of poverty and pain. All the time, there are triumphs in human relationships, when we recognize our own and other people's loneliness and friendship and understanding fill the gaps between us. 'Religion', A. N. Whitehead said, 'is what a man does with his solitariness.' Again and again, the unseen Spirit is at work in homes and in labs, in schools and in colleges, outside God's church but within God's world.

One of the greatest modern painters, Vincent van Gogh, worked out this truth in his own life. As a young Dutchman, he was moved by the suffering of Dutch miners and industrial workers. He became an evangelist, went into the mines, and preached the gospel. His negative experiences led him to think that this was not the way for him to serve God. So he became the artist who has given so much insight wherever his paintings are seen. Van Gogh never forgot the miners or his sense of mission, and developed his powerful style with the deliberate intention that it should be easy to reproduce. Writing to his brother, Theo, he said that in the old days it had been believed that we should paint saints with the haloes round their heads – as it were, obvious sanctity, as you see in the windows of this church. But today, we must paint saints with the haloes inside their heads, inside their eyes. This is what he achieved, both in his paintings of people and of God's extraordinary world. God is hidden in his creation, just as the divine incarnation was hidden in Jesus Christ of Nazareth.

You don't have to go from Norwich to Capernaum or

Massachusetts or the paintings of Van Gogh to discover the truth of Christ's astonished statement, 'I have not found such faith, not even in Israel'. Twenty years ago, the cathedral was re-roofed. The two nave aisles were given fresh oak from Norfolk farms and estates, all donated and all seasoned for ten years at Wroxham. A high level of craftsmanship was needed to use this oak with a lead roof above it, and this was provided by the firm of R. G. Carter under the foreman in those days, John Farrow. There were many complications in this heavy and exposed work, which required great skill. There were many interruptions from services and organ practices. The lead workers did not like the organ practices. They threatened to drop buckets of cement down the organist's pipes.

In 1973, twenty workmen arrived at the Deanery. I was sure it was a strike. I invited them all in to talk things over, but they had come in fact to present a carved lamp made from decayed stone that had had to be removed. When this year the 900th celebrations were organized, these same men asked particularly that there should be a special service for the craftsmen who had kept the cathedral roof secure. Naturally, the cathedral authorities said yes. Perhaps Israel should often wait until the faith that has been evoked outside Israel asks for the moment of prayer, the time to worship.

Many Christian parents wish that their friends and relatives were within Israel, when in fact their children and grand-children do not occupy pews and say that church services are boring. Perhaps we often fail to see what the younger generation are doing to make the world more compassionate, more prosperous, better educated, more able to use science for the common good. There is concealed faith in many of these enterprises. They should not be written off as outside the concern of the Spirit, or lives to which God is indifferent. There is something to celebrate in so many of the endeavours of the younger generation. (See Church of England, General Synod Board for Social Responsibility, *Something to Celebrate: Valuing Families in Church and Society*, Church House Publishing, 1995.)

The story of Christ and the centurion suggests that we should keep our eyes open for faith which may astonish us. We should not let things slide but, as Christ's faithful work as teacher and healer was heard alone by the centurion, we should be quietly confident that the life of the church, the new Israel, has its place in God's plan for the evolution of our world. We are a developing community, praying and living and growing, united by a common belief in Jesus Christ and in the possibility of new life. These are all mysteries. Our task is to remain confident that, if we are alert, we shall see God in many hidden ways. God evokes faith right outside church and temple, synagogue and shrine. Then we shall share Christ's astonishment, 'I have not found such faith, no, not in Israel'.

23. HANDEL

(A sermon preached in Rochester Cathedral by The Very
Revd John Arnold (Dean of Rochester, 1978–89, and Dean
of Durham, 1989–) on the occasion of the tercentenary of
the birth of George Frederic Handel in 1985)

And the glory of the Lord
shall be revealed
ISAIAH 40.5

In the South Quire Aisle of Rochester Cathedral, you will
find a memorial window showing a representation of King
David, over a text which reads 'David took a harp in his
hand and played to the Lord'. Above the royal musician, lest
inspiration should fail, a flying angel is thoughtfully holding
up a scroll on which is a phrase of music in modern notation.
Sight readers among you may like to see if they can make out
what it is, but, rather than keep you in suspense, I will tell
you. It is 'Ombra mai fu' from *Xerxes* by George Frederic
Handel, anachronistically ascribed to the tenth century
BC and thus rather ludicrous, but also deeply moving as a
witness to the fact that when in the twentieth century AD an
artist in stained glass wished to offer to God his sacrifice of
praise and thanksgiving he should without hesitation,
without irony and, we may suppose, practically without
thinking at all, have felt that Handel's 'Largo' was the right
thing to use. Attendants at crematoria, when switching on the
canned Muzak for the committal, think so too; even brides
sometimes, choosing for the only time in their life the music
for a solemn service, agree with this judgement. It is, when
you come to think of it, an astonishing tribute to the spiritual
power and prestige of this naturalized Englishman from
Saxony that his setting of a ridiculous 'ode to a plane tree', in

what turned out to be a rather unsuccessful Italian opera about a pagan Persian king, should be chosen by so many and such varied people as the vehicle for the expression of the joys and sorrows of their own hearts. Handel's music is universal, that is to say it is simultaneously high culture and popular art, in the same way that the works of Homer and Shakespeare, and of very few others, are, that rare breed of whom it can be said, as in Ecclesiasticus (Ecclesiasticus 44.5, 7, 14), 'Some were composers of music or writers of poetry. They were the pride of their times . . . and their name lives for ever.' Such art is beyond analysis; it partakes of the nature of sacraments, whereby spiritual realities are conveyed in physical forms, and it is to be received with thanksgiving rather than criticized or even praised. Let me, instead, say something about Handel, the man.

First, he was a good layman, an undoubted Christian of a rather straightforward and uncomplicated kind. There is nothing clerical or even, compared with his great contemporary Johann Sebastian Bach, of the church musician about him, nothing ecclesiastical at all. Once he had found his own mature voice, his natural arena was not the church, but the world, and the world at its worldliest – London, a city of rich merchants, the seat of the most powerful court in Europe, and the setting, transplanted onto its stages, of Italian opera at the height of its development. Later practice and the piety of later ages should not blind us to the fact that Londoners attended Handel's sacred oratorios, not as a form of church-going but as an alternative to the opera, of which by decree of the Bishop of London they were deprived in Lent. This should not shock us as much as it shocked our Victorian forebears, for, as St John teaches us, God loved *the world* and it is into the *world* that he sends His Word, pre-eminently in His only-begotten Son, but also through His servants the Prophets, and, we may claim, artists in every age.

Handel's mother was the daughter of a Protestant pastor; and he was formed, more than anything else, by her simple, warmhearted and orthodox Lutheran piety. Her memory remained with him all his life; he made her faith his own and remained faithful to it, always refusing politely but firmly to become a Roman Catholic, when in Italy that would have been the gateway to a dazzling and lucrative career. He never formally became a member of the Church of England when he settled in London, although he did become a naturalized British subject by Act of Parliament; but in those days – before the Oxford Movement – Anglicans and Lutherans enjoyed an unselfconscious sense of fellowship which has only recently been regained. He attended his parish church of St George, Hanover Square, every Sunday, even when he was blind and ill, until he could go no more; and he was regular in the exercise of the duties of religion as understood in the early eighteenth century. He was, so far as he was able, liberal to charities and in particular to the Foundling Hospital, for the benefit of which the *Messiah* was performed. Married to music, Handel had no children of his own; but the foundlings filled that place in his affections.

Above all, though, Handel is an exemplary layman, in that he traded vigorously and exclusively with the one talent with which he had been entrusted. He affords a quite exceptional example of enormous mental, physical and spiritual energy, all channelled into one course, and that composition. For Handel this meant celibacy, even though there was nothing of 'the senseless women-hating crew' about him. He liked women and women liked him; but throughout a life-time lived at the raciest levels of London society no breath of scandal ever touched him. This astonishing total self-dedication to one thing, this ability to deny oneself and take up one's cross for the sake of one thing needful, is surely Christ-like, if only in a distant and humble likeness. The composition of the *Messiah* in 24 days, without sleep and practically without food and drink, is the most notable example of concentrated creativity in the history of art, that is to say, in the story of mankind, again comparable, though at a proper distance, with the story of the creation of the world by God in six days.

Secondly, Handel is an example of the sovereignty of God's election, or untrammelled choice of men and women to be

His servants. No amount of research can show good reason why precisely this man should have been gifted in this way. He had no musical ancestry, unlike Bach or for that matter Scarlatti, whom we also celebrate this year. They are like Aaronic priests in the Old Testament, born into long lines of service. He is like a priest after the order of Melchizedek, with neither parentage nor progeny, but chosen directly by God. Unlike the scions of the great musical dynasties, he represents the artistic potentiality of all men in Adam, the fundamental priesthood of man, created to give expression to the thankfulness of creation to its creator. It is this eucharistic priesthood, as the Letter to the Hebrews teaches us, which Jesus assumes, not the levitical priesthood under the law. It is into this priesthood that we are all baptized; and great artists remind us of the splendour of our calling.

But if Handel comes to us unexpectedly out of the blue in provincial Halle, he takes upon himself a tradition, or rather three traditions: the Lutheran church music which old Zachow taught him in the organ loft of the Liebfrauenkirche, the church music and opera of the Italian city states and the musical life of the court, the city and the great churches of London, especially the English verse anthem as perfected by Purcell. (Handel, who had no false modesty but rather the true humility which shewed itself in a just appraisal of his own and other people's worth, Handel when old and blind was once attending a performance of his own *Jephtha* and, when it was compared to Purcell, 'O Gott te teffel', he said – to his dying day he swore in German – 'If Purcell had lived, he would have composed better music than this'.) Handel took what these three traditions offered him and everyone; but it was given to him alone, after the sacramental example of Our Lord Jesus Christ, to take them and give thanks for them, break them and give them back transformed to a new usefulness and splendour.

At the celebration of the sacraments, as at the sight of beauty or the performance of solemn music, it is sometimes given to mortal men to have the veil drawn back and to glimpse from afar the majesty of God and the good things which he has in store for those who love Him, like St Stephen 'to behold by faith the glory that shall be revealed'. When Handel had completed Part II of the *Messiah* with what has come to be known as the 'Hallelujah' chorus, his servant found him at his table in tears; and he exclaimed in his comical, heavily accented Germanic English, 'I did think I did see all heaven before me and the great God Himself'. May he now enjoy the fullness of the vision of God, and know even as he is known; and after his long labours may he rest in peace. Amen.

24. DUKE ELLINGTON

(A sermon preached in Durham Cathedral on Saturday, 6 October 1990, by The Very Revd Dr Peter Baelz, on the occasion of the celebration of the Eucharist to the music of Duke Ellington)

An ancient name by which Christians of the early Church in the West were known was 'Offerentes', or Offerers. The bread and wine, which in the Eucharist they offered to God that it might become for them bread of life and cup of salvation, symbolized both the fruit of the earth and the work of human hands, original gift of the Creator and responsive gift of the creature. The offering of Christ himself, the one perfect offering, grounded eternally in God's free grace, was itself a mutual giving, from God to humankind and from humankind to God.

There is something deep within the human spirit which wants to offer, to give of its utmost and best, not so much to celebrate human achievement – '*do not rejoice that the spirits submit to you*' – as to signify the presence of ultimate mystery – '*but that your names are enrolled in heaven*'. Colloquially, and with a nice sense of inverted reverence, we can speak of doing something, for example, making music, 'for the sheer hell of it' – or, more appropriately, whether for this occasion or for truth itself, '*for the greater glory of God*'.

Among his most significant offerings, Duke Ellington numbered those which he composed for his Sacred Concerts. In a foreword to the first of these concerts, given in Grace Cathedral, San Francisco, in 1965, he wrote:

I believe that no matter how highly skilled a drummer or saxophonist might be, that if this is the thing he does best, and he offers it sincerely from the heart in – or as

104

an accompaniment to – his worship, he will not be un-
acceptable because of lack of skill or of the instrument
upon which he makes his demonstration, be it pipe or
tomtom.

And more than once he made reference to the story of God's
juggler who, having no skills in music or in song, offered the
only skill he had, and in the silence of an empty church stood
before the high altar and juggled to the greater glory of God
– as well as to the astonishment of a chance observer.

Priests of creation – that is what men and women are called
to be. Not its lords, nor its slaves, but its priests. In Paul's
powerful imagery, 'the whole created universe in all its parts
groans as if in the pangs of childbirth', for it 'is waiting with
eager expectation for God's sons to be revealed', and so 'to
enter the glorious liberty of the children of God' (Romans
8.21). In discerning, developing and sharing our gifts of
nature and grace, we align ourselves with the creative and
redemptive purposes of the One whom we call God and, in
offering them in worship, we participate in God's continuing
work of making creation whole and holy.

One of God's greatest gifts to us, a delight for the mind and
a solace for the heart, is the gift of music. The story is told
of the great twentieth-century Swiss theologian, Karl Barth,
how that every day, before settling down to write yet another
chapter of his *magnum opus*, *Church Dogmatics*, he would
listen for an hour to the music of Mozart. When the angels,
he once said, play to the glory of God, they play the music of
Bach. But when they play for their own delight, they play the
music of Mozart. And then the good Lord stops whatever he
happens to be doing in order to listen!

I suggest that the good Lord is taking time off also this
evening to listen to the music of Ellington. May I try to
explain why.

The music of Bach, I suppose, is the official music of
heaven because it combines an almost timeless mathematical
order with a spontaneity of improvisation. The music of
Mozart, however, Barth maintains, is more appropriate to

our condition here on earth, where hope struggles with despair, joy with sorrow, good with evil. Mozart lived and composed at a time following upon the Lisbon earthquake, when the goodness of God was subjected to widespread attack, and (in Barth's own words) 'theologians and other well-meaning folk were hard put to defend him'. In the face of this challenge to God, the music of Mozart (again in Barth's words)

> had the peace of God which far transcends all the critical or speculative reason that praises and reproves . . . He had heard, and causes those who have ears to hear, even to-day, what we shall not see until the end of time – the whole context of providence. As though in the light of this end, he heard the harmony of creation to which the shadow also belongs but in which the shadow is not darkness, deficiency is not defeat, sadness cannot become despair, trouble cannot degenerate into tragedy and infinite melancholy is not ultimately forced to claim undisputed sway.

Mozart contains the light and darkness of the created order in a celebration of faith and hope. What of Ellington?

In a nutshell – for I do not want to outstay my welcome – Ellington's music is rooted in a human story, the story of his people. It is a music of memory and hope – just as the community of Christian faith is a community of memory and hope. It looks back to its origins in the history of black America, and it looks forward to its fulfilment in a community of free women and men. Ellington himself said: 'The memory of things gone is important to a jazz musician. Things like the old folks singing in the moonlight in the backyard on a hot night, or something someone said long ago.' And again: 'Then I try to go forward a thousand years. I seek to express the future when, emancipated and transformed, the Negro takes his place, a free being, among the peoples of the world.' Ellington's music is earthed in the bodies and souls of his people and in their history; but it holds within itself the hope and promise of transformation, of a new heaven and a new earth. Finding its own place at a particular time and in a particular culture, it nevertheless speaks universally to the human condition. And, so speaking, it takes its proper place in a universal sacrifice of praise and thanksgiving, as it does today, here and now, for you and me.

Blessed are you, Lord God of all creation. Through your goodness we have bread to offer, which earth has given and human hands have made. It will become for us the bread of life.

Blessed are you, Lord God of all creation. Through your goodness we have wine to offer, fruit of the vine and work of human hands. It will become our spiritual drink.

Blessed are you, Lord God of all creation. Through your goodness we have music to offer, harmony of human memory and hope. May it become for us food of love, through him who for love of humankind gave his life on the Cross, and lives and reigns with the Father and the Holy Spirit, one God, now and for ever. Amen.

25. ARCHBISHOP WORLOCK

(A sermon preached on 1 March 1996 by The Right Revd Crispian Hollis, Roman Catholic Bishop of Portsmouth, at the Mass for Archbishop Derek Worlock, in his cathedral. Bishop Hollis was the Administrator of Clifton Cathedral, 1981–87)

I was very sad that I was away when Archbishop Derek died and I was doubly sad not to have been able to attend his funeral in Liverpool. It is, therefore, particularly good to have this opportunity today of gathering with so many of you, his friends, brother priests and deacons and former colleagues, to pay him tribute, to thank God for his ministry as priest and bishop and to pray for the repose of his soul.

I think Archbishop Derek would have been glad to know that I was in Bamenda, our sister diocese in Cameroon, when he died. We heard the news early in the morning of the day he died, just as we were preparing to celebrate Mass. That Mass and our prayers were for him, and they were offered in the setting of a Portsmouth missionary endeavour, pioneered and set up by him in 1974. In the days that followed his death, it was indeed moving to hear the tributes being paid to one who had become known in Bamenda as 'the number two bishop'. He is well remembered by the Christian community there and they, led by their Archbishop, have always been immensely grateful to him and to the Portsmouth Diocese for establishing and sustaining the link between the two dioceses.

I reflected at the time that his commitment to mission in its broadest sense was an integral part of his vision of the church. There was little that was parochial in the way in which he saw the Catholic community. It was always seen to be part of a worldwide community with worldwide responsibilities.

His work, both as priest and bishop, was always rooted in the heart of the structures of the church – at Westminster as secretary to three successive cardinals, during the Vatican Council and subsequently as bishop, both here and in Liverpool.

Of all the English bishops in place at the end of the council, Bishop Derek was most prominent in both preaching the Good News of the Council and in his forthright and deliberate determination to implement the spirit of renewal, which flowed from the Council's decrees, into the life of the local church.

It was he who fostered and pioneered the involvement of the laity in the life and work of the church, not least in the structures of parish, deanery and diocesan pastoral councils, the building-blocks of successful collaborative ministry.

In this diocese, he initiated and encouraged the ordination of permanent deacons, of whom Pat Taylor, who read the Gospel today, is a living witness.

It was Bishop Derek who put flesh on the bones of the emerging ecumenical structures after the Council, when that whole world was so very new to most of us. We were able to see and rejoice in the fruit that was to be borne later in his life, most particularly in the very special relationship he enjoyed with Bishop David Sheppard in Liverpool and, more nationally, in the establishment and nurture of Churches Together in England and the Council of Churches of Britain and Ireland.

Within the Bishops' Conference, he was a tower of strength and experience. A new bishop could be sure that the first letter of congratulations on appointment would be post-marked 'Liverpool' and would contain words of congratulations and welcome. It is said that he was 'the memory of the Conference'; either as secretary or as bishop, he scarcely missed a meeting from 1946 until Low Week last year, when he attended for the last time. He made an immense contribution to the emergence of the Catholic community as a force in the land.

It would, perhaps, not be unfair to describe him as a 'fixer', though I am not sure he would be very happy with that word. He was always ready to take on any challenge, whether secular or theological, and his thoroughness and meticulous attention to detail stood him in marvellous stead. This continued almost to the end as evidenced by his leading of the painstaking and complicated negotiations with the Inland Revenue over the tricky question of priests' income tax payments.

But, in many ways, his strengths, evident as they were in his work within the structures of the church, were at their best and most fruitful in his work as a diocesan bishop.

He was particularly a bishop for his priests, though he perhaps found that difficult to express. He encouraged them, he fought for them, he shepherded them with care and devotion – and he loved them. At national level, he did his utmost to ensure that priests had a voice, and energetically supported the National Conference of Priests which provided just such a forum.

As a diocesan bishop, he was acutely conscious of the dignity and role of the lay person and this was something which sprang from his earliest days as a priest and from his work with the YCW (Young Catholic Workers). He was adamant that Catholic laity – men and women – should have a voice in the work and deliberations of local and national government as well as in the church. He backed them up with his own deep involvement in the civic and day-to-day life of the people he served.

Archbishop Derek was, all in all, a great conciliar bishop and churchman. But all these achievements of which I have spoken – and there are many more – were underpinned and underwritten by the life, often hidden, of the man of God. Such a man was vulnerable and sensitive; he needed the affection and love of friends; and, above all, he was always driven and led by the love of Christ, which was, for him, the Way, the Truth and the Life.

There is no doubt about the suffering of his last months and, in the end, he was eager to be set free. He lived – and died – with a vibrant hope of salvation, but, in his suffering, he was content to wait on the Lord with persevering confidence.

Our prayer today is one of thanksgiving for his life and ministry among us, but, at the same time, we pray that he may take possession very soon of one of the many mansions that the Lord has prepared for those who love him. May he rest in peace.

26. THE PERSECUTED CHURCH

(A sermon preached at St Albans Cathedral on the occasion
of the dedication of the Altar of the Persecuted Church on
24 March 1981 by The Very Revd Dr Alan Webster, Dean of
Norwich 1970–78, Dean of St Paul's, 1978–87)

How blest are those who know their need of God; the kingdom
of heaven is theirs. How blest are those who hunger and
thirst to see right prevail; they shall be satisfied. How blest are
those who have suffered persecution for the cause of right;
the kingdom of heaven is theirs.
MATTHEW 5.3, 6 and 10 – *New English Bible*

Tonight, we remember Archbishop Oscar Romero of San
Salvador on the first anniversary of his death. He was shot
while celebrating Mass. We commemorate too all those who
have held to the faith under persecution, from St Alban of
this cathedral to the martyrs of Uganda and Iran.

When I go to church at St Paul's, there stands in a case on
the wall opposite the statue of John Donne this simple letter
from an Anglican priest, Vivian Redlich, dated July 1942. He
was writing home to his father, Basil Redlich, the New
Testament scholar, then a country parson in the Midlands.
The letter runs like this. The address is 'somewhere in the
Papuan Bush'.

> My dear Dad,
> The war has busted up here. I got back from Dogura
> and ran right into it and am now somewhere in my
> parish trying to carry on, though my people are horribly
> scared . . .
> I am trying to stick whatever happens. If I don't come
> out of it, just rest content that I have tried to do my job

faithfully. Rush chance of getting word out, so forgive brevity.

God bless you all,
Vivian

It is believed that Vivian Redlich, a young Anglican missionary in Papua, was killed with his wife on the beach soon after writing this letter.

But tonight we are not concerned with history, not even with the history of heroes. We are here to rejoice in the fact that we are people of the beatitudes and that those extraordinary sayings, which shine above us as we find them either in St Matthew or St Luke, point to the light of Christ. We are people who, for strange, unknown reasons, belong to the company for whom the beatitudes are the marching orders. Tonight, we are not concerned primarily with events in San Salvador or Papua New Guinea or in the early centuries of British Christianity at Verulamium. We are here, around this altar, to become people of the beatitudes. The stories of the peacemakers of our own time, who gave their lives to make peace, Dag Hammarskjöld in Central Africa, Martin Luther King in the United States, encourage us to share the task. An altar is not a place of commemoration; it is a central place for communion and for offering ourselves, our souls and bodies, in a reasonable, holy and lively sacrifice.

Romero did not want to be a martyr. Most of the time, most of us do not want to be unpopular or odd or even to have attention drawn to us in any way. Remember, persecution begins inside our own minds. All those smooth establishment attitudes are already at work, turning us into conformists, whether it is religious conformists, or political conformists, or just people who conform to the easiest way of life. T. S. Eliot's *Murder in the Cathedral*, in its account of the different Tempters who assail Becket, is objectifying in his characters what goes on in the human mind when we are tempted to join a party and be yes-men. It may be a Protestant party or a Catholic party, a political party or a national party. Tonight is a moment of self-examination to discover within ourselves, we folks who do not want to suffer, how far we are resisting the temptations to conformity. Romero did not, Christ did not, Bonhoeffer did not want to become a martyr. We do not. But Christ is alive in people, even, we must pray, within ourselves, when we resist the world, the flesh and the devil inside ourselves and dare to achieve a new consciousness, dare to take our place among the people of the beatitudes.

Romero's family were poor people, and amongst them and their friends the struggle continues. Today, the people of the beatitudes, though we may know them by isolated acts of heroism, are often a community. How much did Romero's mother or his brothers and sisters or just the poor of San Salvador contribute to his heroism? The staff and students of Louvain University, which Romero visited in 1980, strengthened his conviction that the theology of liberation, the bias to the poor, must guide him. How much is contributed today by young people at school who stand for what they believe and suffer in consequence? How much does the church owe to those, usually in completely secular occupations, who make sure that the inefficient are not penalized by society more than they are in any case in a competitive, money-orientated world?

At St Paul's, we know that financiers are needed in the City who will support Nelson Mandela in prison for fighting against apartheid in South Africa, and insist that he should be listened to. They should criticize massive British investment in Southern Africa. Christians in the City should support the friends of Steve Biko, killed by South African police in 1977. International Defence and Aid sends money from its office in Amen Court to support the Mandela and Biko families.

The beatitudes are the most difficult part of the New Testament for all Christians, especially for those who belong to large, wealthy, established churches, such as the Church of England. We easily turn our backs on radical spirituality, radical personal or political demands, It will not do to reject the Nuclear Campaigners unless we are prepared first to listen to and consider their arguments and ourselves seek a way to peace. The Church of England and its great institutions, like cathedrals at St Albans or St Paul's, can miss the real bite of the blessing on the peacemakers. It is not a blessing on the peaceable, though we all need to learn that virtue. It's not a blessing on the compromisers, though we all require the gift of tolerance. It is a blessing of those who so hunger and thirst that they can create peace. Peacemakers are strikingly described in the French *Bible de Jérusalem* as 'Les artisans de paix'.

We must face the conflicts involved in the way the Spirit chooses to work in our world. Here, Søren Kierkegaard, that extraordinary Danish Christian, stands among the prophets. He pointed to thesis and antithesis, a struggle if there is to be synthesis. Kierkegaard, a martyr to his own personality, used to say that 'Where the adamantine gates of hell are at their highest, there must the forces of God be gathered together'.

Women in the church may believe that they have a vocation to the priesthood and ask that it should be tested. Women in local government, especially in the City of London, ask why there has never been a woman Lord Mayor. There are many frontiers which must be crossed if peace is to be made in British life. We are allowing too many disagreements to persist, which damage our society.

Will the Church of England be seen as one of the principal forces which has betrayed our country, failing to tackle difficult questions in its own life and in the life of our nation, and so acting as an ecclesiastical mole for the easy-going side of our institutions and personalities? 'Blessed are those who *make* peace' was the saying of Christ. Martyrs witness that the way to peace is often through facing conflict. The Martyrs' Book at Canterbury Cathedral draws attention to Jonathan Daniels, who died aged 26 still at his theological college, shot dead in the Civil Rights struggle at Haynesville, Alabama, in 1965. Jonathan Daniels is commemorated in the American Episcopal Prayer Book on 14 August as 'Seminarian and Witness for Civil Rights'.

The people of the beatitudes have an ultimate faith that

115

through suffering, which we endure in this evolving planet set in a violent universe, Christ can rise again. As we pursue the journey of our own lives, we may suddenly see a new claim. It may be daunting, and we realize only too clearly the tensions we shall cause when we insist that changes must happen. It is easy to lament the approach of three million unemployed, or the vast armaments industry, or the decline in effective concern for the undernourished, starving people. The test of our faith is so to pray and so to live and so to rejoice in the living God, that we allow Him to give us a little more courage and a little more trust.

We know that the people of the beatitudes are constantly being renewed. That Roman soldier long ago on the hill near here, that young Englishman in the bush in Papua, the battered body of the Archbishop in San Salvador, have shared in the beatitudes which we now pray. May we share their radical obedience and live in hope that we, too, may know the kingdom of heaven, here and hereafter.

Note in 1997

The roll of martyrs has lengthened in many countries since St Albans dedicated its altar in 1981. Five colleagues of Oscar Romero have been assassinated in San Salvador. But peacemaking has continued, especially in South Africa. In England, the Church of England has ordained women to the priesthood, and the City of London has elected its first woman Lord Mayor.

27. ANSELM AND THE WONDER OF GOD

(A sermon preached in Canterbury Cathedral on Sunday, 25 September 1993, on the occasion of the 900th anniversary of the enthronement of St Anselm as Archbishop of Canterbury, by The Rt Revd Dom Philibert Zobel OSB, Abbot of Notre-Dame du Bec-Hellouin)

Readings: 1 Corinthians 2.6–9; Matthew 19.16–21

Your Grace, Brothers and Sisters in Christ.

As we remember St Anselm's enthronement as Archbishop of Canterbury and Primate of All England in this cathedral, 900 years ago, can we forget that he had been, at that time, a monk and an abbot for 33 years in the Abbey of Bec in Normandy? He had himself been a follower of Christ, and he trained his monks to be followers of Christ, to seek God, to discover in prayer and meditation, in obedience and common life, something of the wonder of God who is the Supreme Good.

In the Gospel, we have heard Jesus reminding his disciples that 'one there is who is good!' (Matthew 19.17) From among those who listened to Jesus' teaching, a young man came forward; he asked 'Teacher, what good deed must I do to have eternal life?' He has perceived in the words of the Master, not only the knowledge of the Law but also a presence which opens up a new world before him; he has seen a man, heard a voice which raises the question of the whole meaning and value of his life.

Jesus is the Way to the Father: 'One there is who is good!' And the cost is high: 'If you would be perfect, go, sell what you have and give to the poor. And come, follow me.'

The rich young man dared not take such a step.

St Anselm, after a long struggle, made it. He perceived the wonder of God, the Supreme Good, manifesting and giving himself in His son, Jesus Christ. He gave up everything he had in order to follow Christ on the path of the monastic life, 'which befits those who have nothing dearer than Christ' (Rule of St Benedict).

All through Anselm's life, the wonder of God has been there at work. He remembered his childhood in the Vale of Aosta:

> Being a boy bred among mountains, he imagined that the one God in heaven had his dwelling, his court, on the mountains . . . And one night he saw a vision in which he was bidden to climb to the top of the mountain and hasten to the court of the great King, God . . . and there he was fed with the bread of God.

This call to the vision of God never vanished from his heart. The quest for learning led him from school to school in Burgundy and France, to Normandy and the Abbey of Bec where the famous scholar Lanfranc was teaching. But while he worked hard to master learning, arts and dialectics, the wonder of God, the Father higher than anything, the supreme Good, took possession of his mind and heart.

He went through a hard struggle: would he become a brilliant master, and be acknowledged as a great scholar, or would he surrender to the yearning for this mysterious God, and engage his whole life in the search for him in the monastery? In the end, the wonder of God prevailed: he would become a monk at Bec:

> There I shall have rest, there God only will be my intention, there his love will be the only subject of my contemplation, the blessed and unremitting memory of him will there be my sweet solace and satisfaction.

This does not mean that, from now on, everything would be joy and sweetness. The life and discipline was strict; he had to undertake the demanding work of conversion, to learn obedience, patience, humility, through his shortcomings, the trials of the common life, contradictions, jealousy.

Listening carefully to the word of God in the divine office, silent prayer and meditation, in the reading and study of the Bible (discovering God's presence in community relations with his brother monks) was leading him to an experience of wonder at a deeper level. He could witness God at work in the conversion of a young rebel monk, in opening the minds of young students to the splendour of God's truth. The wonder of the inaccessible light in which the Supreme Good dwells permeated the whole life of the monk, as well as the meditation of the scholar.

Anselm's experience of the wonder of God is still conveyed to us through his theological writings. The yearning to behold the face of God which was moving his whole life of prayer, conversion, obedience and work in the monastic community, was the force which moved his believing thought towards understanding. And if we are set on following his steps, we can still experience something of this wonder. Through the strictness of his dialectical walk, we can feel the yearning to see.

> O Lord God, why does my soul not perceive you, if it has found you? Has it not found someone whom it has found to be light and truth? . . . My soul strains to see more; but beyond what it has already seen, it peers only into darkness. . . . Is the eye of the soul darkened as a result of its own weakness, or is it dazzled by your brilliance?

Anselm no longer strives to grasp God as an object to be possessed. In his intellectual process, we find the same conversion as in his monastic quest. He gives up the desire to possess God, to master his perfection, his knowledge, and he surrenders both his life and his intellectual thrust to the one 'in whom he lives, moves and exists'. He consents to be possessed.

> Therefore, O Lord, not only are You that than which a greater cannot be thought, but You are also something greater than can be thought.

He has found that *that than which a greater cannot be thought* must exist not only in the mind but also in reality. But if he would seize it, his hands would only grasp wind. He has to let *the One who is greater than can be thought* seize him.

Such an approach to God, to reality, may no longer be familiar to us. Anselm goes from faith to faith, from a dark faith which receives in obedience the revealed truth from the scriptures in the church to a free adhesion enlightened by intelligence, recognizing both the demands and the limits of reason.

Reason searches for coherence and necessity in the revealed truth: God exists; by him, the Supreme Good, everything exists and is good; he is Father, Son and Spirit; the Son of God was made man and reconciled with God creation alienated by sin . . .

Moving forward step by step into the understanding of divine truth, Anselm comes to a point where he must exceed all comprehension and admit that his thought is totally unable to understand the mystery of God. In the night of Unknowing, he discovers himself to be surrounded on every part by the infinite splendour of God, which he is only able to behold in admiration and wonder.

How difficult indeed for us, this surrender, this going beyond all our logical certainties. We are used to a critical approach to reality, to methodological doubt; the search for certainty, or at least for probability, leads us to put aside as irrational that which exceeds our comprehension. Moreover, the desire to experience reality, to master this experience, prevents us from surrendering to the wonder of the mystery of God, ever greater, ever better than can be thought and experienced.

Anselm can give us an idea of the fruitfulness of this surrendering to the wonder of God; his theological arguments do not cease to fascinate modern philosophers, who can never put them aside as irrelevant or meaningless.

Is it not also this sense of the wonder of God which has led Anselm to such uprightness and rectitude of will in discerning the will of God? It was the case when against all human desires he had to consent to his election as Archbishop of Canterbury.

In his theological researches, as well as in the struggles for the liberty of the church, he never ceased to try to adjust the eye of his mind and heart, still weak and darkened, to the dazzling light of the mystery of God.

Therefore, O Lord, the whole of Your joy will not enter into those who are rejoicing; instead they will enter into Your joy.

Speak, O Lord, and tell Your servant in his heart whether this is the joy into which Your servants will enter, when they will enter into the joy of their Lord. Now surely no eye has seen, no ear has heard, nor has there entered into the heart of man – that joy in which Your elect ones will rejoice. (*Proslog.* 26)